ORWELL'S FICTION

ORWELL'S FICTION

Robert A. Lee

UNIVERSITY OF NOTRE DAME PRESS

NOTRE DAME   LONDON

For Gloria

Acknowledgments

Permission to reprint excerpts from Orwell's *Burmese Days*, *A Clergyman's Daughter*, *Keep the Aspidistra Flying*, *Homage to Catalonia*, *Coming Up For Air*, *Animal Farm*, and *1984* was granted by Brandt & Brandt, Harcourt, Brace & World, Inc., Miss Sonia Brownell and Secker & Warburg. Permission to reprint excerpts from Orwell's *Collected Essays* was granted by Secker & Warburg and Miss Sonia Brownell and by Harcourt, Brace & World. Permission to reprint excerpts from Irving Howe's *Orwell's 1984: Text, Sources, Criticism* was granted by Harcourt, Brace & World. I acknowledge with thanks these permissions. Somewhat different versions of Chapter I and Chapter VI appeared in, respectively, *Texas Studies in Literature and Language* and *Studies in Short Fiction*. I acknowledge the kind permission of the editors of these journals to reprint.

This study has seen many versions and I wish to acknowledge the aid and advice of several people who have read it in various forms. I am most in debt to the wisdom and tolerance of A. K. Weatherhead and the late Frederick J. Hoffman. The advice of these two men saved me from egregious errors of fact on several occasions, as well as from countless lapses in taste. To both these gentlemen I am in debt for far more than their aid on this book. The errors and flaws that remain are, of course, my own. I also wish to acknowledge assistance given at various times by Christof Wegelin, Waldo McNeir, and William Cadbury. And I must make a special acknowledgment of gratitude to Miss Emily Schossberger and Miss Betty Prevender of the University of Notre Dame Press.

The final version of this book was completed while I was a Fellow of the Center for Advanced Study of the University of Illinois. To the University and to the Center's director, David Pines, I am deeply indebted for several kinds of assistance. To the seemingly countless typists and research assistants who have at one time and in one way or another helped me on this project I extend thanks and apologize for the anonymity this kind of acknowledgment demands.

Finally, my greatest debt is to my wife, to whom this book is dedicated, and who has endured far beyond the call of necessity in living with George Orwell and me over the past several years.

R. A. L.

Contents

Introduction

Lionel Trilling's moving anecdote of how he and one of his students were affected by George Orwell, how they found pleasure in just sitting and quietly thinking about that "virtuous man," is symptomatic of the way in which critics have come to consider Orwell. A common critical approach seems to be the epithet: To some he is "decent"; to some a "saint"; to others "the conscience of his generation." Indeed, it is difficult to read extensively in Orwell's work without coming away with some such feeling. There emanates from his writing a sense of sanity welcome in an age that often seems insane; he reveals a personality most attractive in its reasonableness, its kindness—virtues in which modern life seems notably lacking. And even when Orwell is not revealing a kind of common-sense perception, but is instead apocalyptic and visionary, as in 1984, his prophecies seem to have been so closely borne out by time, ironically so "sensible," that again one's reaction is admiration for the man who could conceive so precisely and accurately our immediate future. In short, Orwell is much admired—by persons of widely differing political views—as a man, as an essayist, as a political thinker.

Orwell's force as a political commentator has been so pervasive that his art has suffered a unique fate: When his fiction is considered, in a curious reversal of normal critical procedure it is often used only to gloss his nonfiction. The novels are usually disdained. Richard Rovere, an admiring and sympathetic critic and the editor of a selection of Orwell's work, The Orwell Reader, passes what are common judgments: Though a writer of "great force and distinction," Orwell is a "minor" novelist; though never second-rate he is "of the second rank"; his work does not lend itself to criticism; the meanings of his novels are "mostly on the surface." Of Orwell's six novels, only 1984 has received as much consideration as the essays, and even this book has been examined mostly for its "ideas" rather than as a novel. I wish to redress the balance and to consider Orwell as a novelist. For this reason I have deliberately refrained from full-length discussions of two of Orwell's most interesting books, *Down and Out in Paris and London* and *The Road to Wigan Pier*, although they contain nearly all the elements that appear in his fiction. For the major problems these books suggest —poverty and its effect on the spirit and the discrepancy between public demands and private desires—are, I think, better revealed by a reading of Orwell's novels. I have, for a similar reason, tried to keep to a minimum references to Orwell's essays, so many of which are repeatedly anthologized. The temptation is too great—and too easily misleading with a man who wrote so many essays on so many topics—to resolve every problem a novel raises by a reference to Orwell's own, straightforward voice.

I propose that the novels reveal the political insights—if that is what we are to look for in Orwell—in a more fully developed way than do his nonfictional writings. I will suggest a clear development in Orwell's career as early, inchoate ideas become gradually refined, mediated, and deepened. Orwell's novels reveal his progress from an individual, contained, largely parochial response to social problems to an apocalyptic vision which attempts to come to terms with the most significant and wide-ranging issues of our time. This is not to say that the last novels are necessarily superior to the early ones. In fact, according to the standards of the fully created, coherent, significant world which we expect in a novel, I suggest that Orwell's first novel, *Burmese Days*, is in many ways the best.

But there is much to be said for the notion that one must consider the significance of the theme of the work, and that an ambitious or profound failure is more important than a piece of limited perfection. Orwell's development to more important moral and social issues in the late works suggests my second major intention: I will contend that what turned Orwell from a minor to a major novelist was the Spanish Civil War, Orwell's involvement in it, and his insights growing from it. In his first three novels, *Burmese Days* (1934), *A Clergyman's Daughter* (1935), and *Keep the Aspidistra Flying* (1936), Orwell pursued a conventional theme—the problem of the individual conscience versus public demands —in contexts portraying a wide spectrum of the social and political life of England and Englishmen between wars. In all three books the focus is private. How does the individual accommodate society? What are the livable terms under which private virtue is modified for the public weal? After his experiences in Spain—detailed in *Homage to Catalonia*, the one nonfictional work which I examine in detail—the concern is still for the individual, but the nature of society has been newly apprehended. The issue is no longer how man can find some kind of workable truce with an inevitably demanding community, but whether or not man can preserve his own self in the face of an overwhelming state. These political insights are, I suggest, discovered primarily in Spain and are directly translated to the world of his fiction following Spain.

Those political insights are expressed mainly through the increasingly important theme of corrupted language. In the earliest books the application is primarily one of communication. In *Burmese Days*, language fails at crucial moments in ways which suggest that merely to articulate, to establish communication, would be sufficient to prevent disaster. The worst fate the individual can face is isolation; simply to talk is to reject such a fate, and is thus to be saved. At this point, Orwell does not seem to care overmuch about the kind of society into which one is saved. The community of *Burmese Days* is so corrupt and contemptible that the reader is likely to feel that the protagonist's suicide is a preferable alternative to life in such a world. But the novel makes clear enough, I think, that Orwell does not share such a view and that we are meant to see this suicide as a wrong choice. The heroine of Orwell's next novel, faced with very much the same problem, chooses differently, and her acceptance of her life seems to be Orwell's deliberately cast alternative to the resolution of his first book. If more positive in its resolution, A Clergyman's Daughter also reveals an increasingly negative approach to the uses of language. This book portrays language as more than simple communication or articulation. There are examples of newspaper distortion, of the deliberate and destructive manipulation of language. One aspect of the plot turns upon a case of petty, provincial censorship. And Keep the Aspidistra Flying, Orwell's next novel, concentrates even more on corrupt and corrupting language. The hero is torn between the callings of poetry and advertising; Orwell suggests the former is perhaps noble, but futile; the latter may be banal but is somehow more real and so more healthy.

However, this summary of Orwell's first three novels suggests a paradox. There is an unmistakable insistence on social acceptance, or coming to terms with the world, no matter its demands, no matter its quality. Yet the terms of society begin to seem too great; variations upon the nature of language increasingly define Orwell's reservations about society. To give up being a bad poet to become a good advertising writer seems a realistic and wise choice. But it is a matter of giving up, and the description of the advertising world raises implications and makes suggestions about subsequent and far more evil uses of language than are found in mere slogan writing. I suggest, simply, that in these first three books Orwell indeed believed that acceptance was better than isolation, and society more important than the self, if such choices had to be made. But at the same time, he was undercutting his own beliefs in the very act of creating the social worlds he was defending. In a sense, he was writing himself out of belief in what he was writing about. Actual confirmation that such belief was wrong comes from his experiences in the Spanish Civil War and is plainly expressed in his rendition of those experiences in Homage to Catalonia.

Orwell's last three novels, *Coming Up For Air*, *Animal Farm* and *1984*, demonstrate both the dramatic repudiation of his former attitudes and his increasing reliance on the uses of language as a way to demonstrate his new insight. Ironic advertising slogans evolve into the seven "commandments" of Animal Farm and finally into Newspeak. Language is no longer seen as the means by which man communicates with his neighbor and is thus able to enter society; it has become a means by which society comes to control man completely. Not the least of the new insights Orwell gains in Spain, and one which he has gradually acquired in the creative self-education of his novels, is a new vision of society. The passive, "useful" qualities which make for a stable community become intolerable servitude, blindly ignorant quiescence in Winston Smith's world. Society is a terror to be avoided, not a refuge to be sought. The realization of self *in* language changes to the denial of all such possibility *through* language. Orwell's nonfiction, again, provides a strong temptation to confirm this reading. But I argue that even so deservedly famous an essay as "Politics and the English Language" does not disclose as much of Orwell's concept of the uses of language as does its thematic incorporation in *1984*.

I do not suggest that the readings of the respective novels that I give here are in any way exhaustive. In fact, I have consciously emphasized different features of the different novels —symbolism in *Burmese Days*, character in *Keep the Aspidistra Flying*, point of view in *Coming Up For Air*—to suggest Orwell's range and artistry. Further, in trying to trace an ordered development in his career, doubtless I have exaggerated certain aspects of each novel and insufficiently treated others. For example, one technique that Orwell employs throughout his career is the use of animal metaphors to suggest human states of behavior. I look at this pattern closely in only one novel. Nor do I treat as fully as I might have the interesting fact that nearly all of Orwell's protagonists are in one way or another "wounded." It seems probable that the psychological implications of this phenomenon could be applied to Orwell's own life. But in fact I argue throughout against biographical criticism of his books. In trying to make a case for the integrity of Orwell's novels, I have had to answer' the previous criticism these novels have received—which is predominantly devoted to the discovery in them of thinly disguised biographical equivalents in Orwell's own experiences. If nothing else, I hope I provide sufficient reason to suggest alternative, but textual, readings.

For my method throughout is unabashedly textual, and it is a method which I feel is particularly necessary for Orwell. In the most recent, and to my thinking easily the best, book on Orwell, The Crystal Spirit, George Woodcock reproves American scholars for the "absurd assiduousness" of their attempts to read closely didactic, polemic writers. No "New Critic," says Woodcock, has successfully "tackled" Swift or Dickens; the same restriction thus applies to Orwell. And though Woodcock himself reads some of the novels quite closely and sensitively, that is not my point. I submit that textual exegesis is the only valid way we can come to assess literature, the only way by which we can judge, and the only way we can accurately understand ideas in imaginative writing, be they polemic, didactic, or esthetic. I concur fully with David Lodge in his Language of Fiction: "Literary critics can claim special authority not as witnesses to the moral value of works of literature, but as explicators and judges of effective communication." Orwell's novels are indeed structures which imply and reveal directly moral, social, and political concerns. But we must make literary judgments before we can understand his ethical or social concepts.

A final word about the political base of Orwell's art. In our time, we seem to have forgotten the political nexus of literature. To a Shakespeare, a Spenser, a Milton, a Wordsworth, politics was an essential part of art. From the 1920's until, at least, our recent involvement in Viet Nam, our literature seems part of an intellectual milieu which more and more renounces social involvement for the private struggles of an inner self. Perhaps Orwell and his relationship with politics and art can reestablish an object lesson for our time. For, despite natural reservations and personal differences of opinion, an extended reading of Orwell's writings must convert anyone, I submit, to acceptance of one of his cardinal tenets: In this century, the artist must contend with the world if either art or politics is to have meaning.

I

BURMESE DAYS

> No man is the lord of anything,
> Though in him and of him there be much consisting,
> 'Till he communicate his parts to others.
> —*Troilus and Cressida*

Burmese Days, Orwell's first novel (published in 1934), is regarded by most critics as simply a polemic against the British Raj. John Atkins, for example, divides Orwell's writings by "subjects," of which the first is "Imperialism."[1] It would be naive to contend that there is no anti-imperialism in *Burmese Days*; but there is more to the novel than political comment. To examine *Burmese Days* on literary grounds, to view the book as a fictive world, is to see that it is a novel built on a series of symbolic patterns, some obvious, some more subtle. Such a method is perhaps typical of a first novel, for symbolism lends to the apprentice novelist a ready-made richness, a kind of convenient shorthand that must be appealing. Dangers lie, of course, in the possible heavy-handedness of the symbology, and it may be that the obvious Freudian bias of the symbols Orwell employs are, for current tastes at least, overdone. But the crucial point is, I think, that such is an *artistic* judgment, and that Orwell's concerns were artistic. The novel is not merely propaganda; it exists other than as a polemic.

The action of the novel is centered on the main character,

1

John Flory; the many intrigues and subplots in one way or another impinge on or derive from his thoughts and actions. Yet for all the subordinate action, the main plot is straightforward. Flory has been a timber manager in the colonial outpost of Kyauktada for fifteen years. More sensitive and intelligent than his fellow *sahibs*, who range from bigot to drunken lecher, he is alienated from his countrymen not only by his superior intellect, but by his willingness to accept, enjoy, and even like the local natives. Thus, though somewhat unwilling, he becomes conscience-bound to try to have the first native admitted into the European Club. This attempt meets with frantic resistance from the other English, and it involves Flory in the intrigues of U Po Kyin, the "Sub-divisional Magistrate," the highest ranking native official. But this is really only the secondary action of the novel. What preoccupies Flory most is Elizabeth Lackersteen, the stupid, jejune niece of one of the other colonists, with whom Flory falls hopelessly in love. The major action of the plot is then devoted to the subsequent successes and failures in Flory's courtship. Finally, his ex-mistress, a Burmese under the control of U Po Kyin, who is hoping to discredit Flory, creates a scene, which scandalizes Elizabeth, who makes a final break with Flory. Following this action, Flory goes home and shoots himself.

This drama is played out against a jungle background, reinforcing the themes of the novel by a subtle symbolic pattern —namely, the linking and contrasting of two jungles, the natural one and the artificial but still beast-filled jungle of the Club. But the dominant symbol in the book is that which most distinguishes Flory, that which he cannot forget, which influences his every action, and which finally becomes responsible for his death:

> The first thing that one noticed in Flory was a hideous birthmark stretching in a ragged crescent down his left cheek, from the eye to the corner of the mouth. Seen from the left side his face had a battered, woebegone look, as though the birthmark had been a bruise—for it was a dark blue in colour. He was quite aware of its hideousness. And

at all times, when he was not alone, there was a sidelong-ness about his movements, as he manoeuvred constantly to keep the birthmark out of sight.[2]

The naevus is, at the simplest level, a physical manifes-tation of his alienation from society. Frederick R. Karl says Flory's birthmark suggests the mark of Cain; it "identifies him and disallows his escaping his fate, which is, obviously, to be marked from birth for some role."[3] Though unspeci-fied by Karl, Flory's "role" is apparently to stand against the cant and hypocrisy of the Club world Because his beliefs are inherently destructive to the Club's values Flory, like Cain, is a vagabond and a wanderer on the face of the earth. But in the world of Kyauktada, alienation is a partially redeeming factor: The birthmark suggests Flory's separateness and thus his superiority to corrupt values and moral lassitude. He alone of all the characters of the novel, English or Burmese, under-stands the effects on the mind of years of colonialist values.

> In the end the secrecy of your revolt poisons you like a secret disease. Your whole life is a life of lies. Year after year you sit in Kipling-haunted little Clubs, whisky to right of you, Pink'un to left of you, listening and eagerly agree-ing while Colonel Bodger develops his theory that these bloody Nationalists should be boiled in oil. You hear your Oriental friends called "greasy little babus," and you admit, dutifully, that they are greasy little babus. You see louts fresh from school kicking grey-haired servants. The time comes when you burn with hatred of your own country-men, when you long for a native rising to drown their Empire in blood. And in this there is nothing honourable, hardly even any sincerity. For, au fond, what do you care if the Indian Empire is a despotism, if Indians are bullied and exploited? You only care because the right of free speech is denied you. You are a creature of the despotism, a pukka sahib, tied tighter than a monk or a savage by an unbreak-able system of tabus. (p. 69)

Flory is made bitter by the corruption around him. Yet his failure to renounce this corruption demonstrates a crucial fault in his character: Insight does not lead to action, and that "unbreakable system" will eventually be the cause of Flory's death. Both strength and weakness are suggested by his birthmark.

The birthmark symbol operates in other ways. On a morning which starts as typical in Kyauktada—a forty-year-old Burmese is beaten by the police; Flory is hungover; Mr. Macgregor, the obtuse Deputy Commissioner, desperately does his morning exercises, "Nordenflycht's 'Physical Jerks for the Sedentary' "[4]—Flory receives a thinly veiled threat from U Po Kyin warning him not to support his Burmese friend, Dr. Veraswami, for election to the Club. Wanting to avoid the issue, Flory is in the process of tearing the letter up, pretending it never reached him, when he hears a sudden, terrified scream. Followed by his dog, he runs around the back of the compound to the jungle.

> Just behind the house, beyond the first fringe of bushes, there was a small hollow, which, as there was a pool of stagnant water in it, was frequented by buffaloes from Nyaunglebin. Flory pushed his way through the bushes. In the hollow an English girl, chalk-faced, was cowering against a bush, while a huge buffalo menaced her with its crescent-shaped horns. A hairy calf, no doubt the cause of the trouble, stood behind. Another buffalo, neck-deep in the slime of the pool, looked on with mild prehistoric face, wondering what was the matter. (pp. 79–80)

The crescent shape of the buffalo's horns reflects the shape of the naevus on Flory's face, and this suggests dramatic irony —as the buffalo is now, Flory later will be a menace to Elizabeth. The menace is defined (hinted at now but made explicit subsequently) by the phallic connotations of the horns. Elizabeth is menaced always by that which is natural, and sex is the most natural force impinging on this attractive, young, and single girl. Ironically, Flory's masculinity is finally to be no threat at all. But at this point, as with the harmless beast in the water, the stress is on Flory's power, his virility, as he saves Elizabeth from danger, in a rather melo-dramatic version of the maiden-in-distress motif. Like the "hairy calf," Flory is heavily bearded; like the buffalo, Flory will become feared for his virility and power; like the animal, he is in reality harmless. He is acceptable now, however, as he will not be later, because now in the natural jungle his naevus is absorbed; his "bestiality" is fitting and even neces-sary. But at the same time as the crescent-shape unites Flory and Elizabeth, there is a suggestion in the use of the symbol, even before we learn of Elizabeth's character, that they are incompatible. For the submersion of the symbol into the jungle world is unique; outside of this natural, incorporating context, the cresent-shape's essentially sexual implications are indeed a threat to Elizabeth. Ultimately, her incompatibility with the natural world becomes final—and the cause of suf-fering and death.

Another recurring image which appears in this scene is the description of Elizabeth as "chalk-faced." In another revealing context in the novel, Ma Hla May, Flory's Burmese mistress, has a "face grey with powder" in the crucial scene where she denounces Flory in the church; the pwe dancer that Flory unwisely and unfortunately takes Elizabeth to see has a face so powdered "it gleamed in the lamplight like a chalk mask with live eyes behind it" (p. 106). Elizabeth, then, is being compared to the natives, whom she abhors and is disgusted by; the difference is that each person is only appropriate in a certain context. If Elizabeth is like Ma Hla May in their common attempt to use Flory for their own ends, she is dif-ferent from the Burmese mistress because she represses her own sexual feelings. The pwe dancer, who wriggles "her two buttocks independently in time with the music" (p. 106), patently represents a sexual candor that contrasts with, and in the process defines, Elizabeth.

The symbol of the birthmark and the image of "chalk-faced" define character through the context of the setting. Elizabeth and Flory are set against various backgrounds which regulate their relationship. In their first meeting, in the jungle where Flory has rescued Elizabeth, his scar absorbed by its surroundings, there is immediate and spontaneous empathy, naturally emphasized by the circumstances of the rescue. The next scene in which they are alone—when Flory takes her to see the *pwe* celebration—ends disastrously. At this point Flory is trying to get Elizabeth to assume a set of values which he holds—acceptance and even fondness for the Burmese—and though there are only marginal distinctions between the native women and Elizabeth, she is nevertheless wholly committed to the values of the Club world. Her conversation ranges from horses to the weather; her intolerance of natives is similar to that of Ellis, the Club bigot, only expressed less violently. Paradoxically similar, the Club world must be distinguished from the real jungle. In the Club, nature is shut out; the natives are barred. There, Elizabeth is at home precisely because the world is artificial and superficial. At the same time the Club is itself a jungle, with its predators and victims hidden behind the veneer of civilized cruelty.

Flory's desire for Elizabeth is doomed: in any other context than the Club, where Flory is suspect because of his unconventional ideas but where her feeble mind is at peace among that world's minimal demands, or the jungle, where Elizabeth can only impermanently live, Flory and Elizabeth cannot get along. The fact that their relatively successful moments in their relationship take place only in the jungle suggests other patterns. At the first remove, this situation is part of what we may call the "bestial" pattern of the novel: The two jungles of the story—the natural one and the Club —show Elizabeth's motives to be essentially animalistic. Only slightly more overt than the predatory way the members of the Club treat each other in that refined atmosphere are Elizabeth's actions in the real jungle. In fact, the latent violence and sadism that all the other characters show is synthesized in her. In a scene similar to their first meeting and in a desperate attempt to break down Elizabeth's disdain, Flory takes her on a hunting trip. In their first meeting, she had revealed an interest in violence and danger that fore-shadows this event: now, when they are talking after his rescue of her, "she was quite thrilled when he described the murder of an elephant which he had perpetrated some years earlier" (p. 85).[5] They are paddled up the river, with Elizabeth "nursing her uncle's gun across her knees," refusing to give it up for safekeeping to Flory (p. 158) in a scene which suggests her sexual frustration, and they move into the jungle to hunt. They see some green pigeons—to which Flory has earlier been likened[6]—and Flory shoots and kills two, a symbolic foreshadowing of his suicide. Immediately, Elizabeth also shoots and kills one, and this seems to represent her later culpability in Flory's death. Both Flory and the pigeon are solitary—one beautiful, one ugly; both find the same fate: Hunted as are animals, they are killed by other beasts in strange jungles.

Elizabeth's reaction to shooting the pigeon clearly reveals her latent capacity for violence and sex—and thus limits the success of their relationship. Flory wants only to "talk."

> She could hardly give it up, the feel of it so ravished her. She could have kissed it, hugged it to her breast. All the men, Flory and Ko S'la and the beaters, smiled at one another to see her fondling the dead bird. Reluctantly, she gave it to Ko S'la to put in the bag. She was conscious of an extraordinary desire to fling her arms around Flory's neck and kiss him; and in some way it was the killing of the pigeon that made her feel this. (p. 167)

The thin line that separates death and sex is obliterated. In metaphorically killing Flory, Elizabeth comes to love him, to have the rhetorical equivalent of sexual intercourse with him. For human, natural desire—that part of her evident in and perhaps released by the jungle—is denied in the hypocritical, artificial world of the Club. Elizabeth and Flory continue the hunt, now for a jungle cock: "they had to bend double to keep themselves out of sight" (p. 167). Once again together in a context of violence and death, they are united, assuming themselves a variation of the crescent-shape as they together become assimilated by the natural jungle. And the ironic equivalent of a post-coital state is attained when true violence and danger are mutually met in the killing of a leopard:

> Elizabeth's shoulder was almost touching Flory's as they walked. The sweat that had drenched their shirts had dried again. They did not talk much. They were happy with that inordinate happiness that comes of exhaustion and achievement, and with which nothing else in life—no joy of either the body or the mind—is even able to be compared. (pp. 173–174)

Following this "it was understood between them that they would meet. Also, it was understood that Flory would ask Elizabeth to marry him, though nothing was said about this either" (p. 174). Importantly, here and elsewhere the promise is not articulated: In effect, language fails, and language implicitly becomes the one means by which man can withstand human animal savagery. This failure is to be Flory's crucial mistake, for just as beasts have brought the two together, so beasts are destined to separate them, temporarily and permanently.

The "bestial" pattern runs throughout the book. On a rather conventional level, for example, there is a comparison of the various humans to animals—a technique that works nicely in this jungle world. Deputy Commissioner Macgregor, pontificating and obtuse, who wants to avoid any trouble rising from the admission of Veraswami to the Club, "reminded one curiously of a turtle" (p. 28).[7] U Po Kyin, plotting and malevolent, so enormously fat that he likes to think of himself as "swollen with the bodies of his enemies" (p. 14) is likened to a crocodile. Ellis, a horrible bigot who tells obscene jokes and smirkingly questions Flory about his relationship with Elizabeth, is "goatish" (p. 110). And Flory becomes, through the similarity in name and through some adroit management of symbol by Orwell, closely linked to his dog, Flo. Thus, one dismal, dreary night prior to Elizabeth's transforming appearance on the scene, Flory, wallowing in self-pity, becomes angered at the wailing of some dogs outside his bungalow.

> Flory went back to the veranda, took up the rifle, and, wincing slightly, let drive at the pariah dog. There was an echoing roar, and the bullet buried itself in the maidan, wide of the mark. A mulberry-coloured bruise sprang out on Flory's shoulder. The dog gave a yell of fright, took to its heels, and then, sitting down fifty yards farther away, once more began rhythmically baying. (p. 73)

Flory, already likened to a dog through Flo, is the pariah in his society.[8] Marked both by his physical appearance and by values which threaten the stability of the Club, he is the outcast from its world. This scene alone, believably integrated into the action, symbolically accurate without straining any metaphors, seems to me to suggest Orwell's artistry even so early in his career.

As all the other members of the Club are beasts, so too is Elizabeth: After Flory saves the Club from the natives' abortive rebellion and he and Elizabeth meet, she relives her happy times with him: "It was the buffalo and the leopard over again. His heart thumped in his breast" (p. 259). Verrall, who has a "rabbit-like" face (p. 184), and Elizabeth dance together in the Club "in perfect unison like some single animal" (p. 210). And after riding together (horses are Verrall's first love—he "sat his horse as though he were part of it"), Verrall and Elizabeth kiss for the first time.

> The next evening, as they rode home side by side, Verrall put his arm around Elizabeth's shoulder, lifted her out of the saddle and pulled her against him. He was very strong. He dropped the bridle, and with his free hand, lifted her face up to meet his; their mouths met. For a moment he held her so, then lowered her to the ground and slipped from his horse. They stood embraced, their thin, drenched shirts pressed together, the two bridles held in the crook of his arm. (p. 215)

It is almost the perfect marriage of man, woman—and beast. Or, to alter the terms only slightly, two beasts are united by—and tied to—two others.

The use of bestial imagery to foreshadow and define action is effectively used elsewhere. Mr. Macgregor is likened, at one point, to a "friendly saurian monster" (p. 110); Elizabeth's aunt, Mrs. Lackersteen, has "delicate, saurian hands" (p. 97). Epitomizing the worlds of the Club and of Elizabeth's parasitic selfishness, respectively, these two lizard-like creatures have their natural counterparts. Early in the book, lying indolently in bed, Flory watches a lizard "stalk a moth above the bookshelves" (p. 55). After Elizabeth's final rejection of him at the church Flory returns home to kill himself:

> He hurriedly tore open his coat and pressed the muzzle of the pistol against his shirt. A tiny lizard, translucent like a creature of gelatine, was stalking a white moth along the edge of the table. Flory pulled the trigger with his thumb. (p. 281)

The lizard finally catches its prey, just as the values of the Club and the solipsistic Elizabeth Lackersteen finally capture Flory. And just before shooting himself Flory, for no apparent reason, kills his dog, Flo. The symbolic threads are drawn together. The pariah dog is finally hit, as both literal and metaphorical outcasts meet their appointed fate. Just so, the moth—that creature related to the beautiful butterfly, but, like Flory, without the redeeming aspect of beauty to justify its otherwise purposeless existence—is caught and destroyed. The jungle world, indifferent to death and birth, claims another victim.

It would seem, then, that the jungle functions in the novel primarily as the locus of violence and death, ironically defining the Club as but another jungle and claiming the victims of its scene.[9] It serves other uses. If the jungle is at one remove the symbolic assailant of John Flory, it is at the same time his sole refuge from the more dangerous jungle of the English colonialists. This strategy is defined mainly through recurring patterns of water imagery, a conventional literary symbol but one which Orwell uses with great facility.

Following a distasteful scene with Ma Hla May which culminates in a degrading act of sexual intercourse, Flory retreats to the jungle, where he first sweats himself "into a better mood." Then going by a trail which "few human beings ever followed," to a pool he knows well he bathes in "clear greenish water." It is a secular baptism, regenerating Flory through nature, cleansing him of the sin and corruption of the world in which he must of necessity live.[10] Alone in the jungle, Flory is revitalized from his swim in clear water. In contrast, Elizabeth is first encountered in the context of a far different quality of water: In the scene already noted, Elizabeth and Flory meet as she is frightened by beasts that stand in "stagnant water" (p. 79). It is this second kind of water that will eventually come to immerse Flory, literally and figuratively. This image is joined with the pattern of animal imagery in a crucial scene. After Flory and Elizabeth return from the hunting trip, which has brought them closer than they will ever be again—and in which they are both drenched in sweat —they meet at the Club and go out to the terrace. Flory delays proposing; as Elizabeth irritably waits for him to do it, he tries to talk to her of his solitude and loneliness. His talking, ironically, delays true communication; she does not care, nor understand what he is trying to say. She wants only the articulated proposal—something which would, in fact, have prevented all the further tragedy. Finally he is about to ask her to marry him:

> "Quickly, there's just time. Answer me this. Will you—"
> But that sentence never got any further. At the same moment something extraordinary happened under his feet —the floor was surging and rolling like a sea—he was staggering, then dizzily falling, hitting his upper arm a thump as the floor rushed towards him. As he lay there he found himself jerked violently backwards and forwards as though some enormous beast below were rocking the whole building on its back. (p. 181)

As a natural beast has brought them together, so another parts them. The "sea" of the Club keeps them apart at the crucial moment, when articulation would have banded them together formally and, in the world of the Club, irrevocably. The *pukka sahib* and *burra memsahib* do not contradict the forms of their society; that is the white man's way.

Flory has one more chance with Elizabeth, once again described in the context of water imagery. Through the big-otry and cruelty of Ellis combined with the plotting of U Po Kyin, the club is assaulted by the villagers of Kyauktada. At this time the relationship of Elizabeth and Flory is at its low-est ebb; the arrogant and disdainful Lieutenant Verrall is courting and, apparently, seducing her—not unwillingly on her part. (The Verrall-virile pun is consonant with the notions of Elizabeth's frustrated sexuality, coy and artless as such name-puns may now seem.) The rebellion originally seems harmless, but the violence of the natives grows, prodded on by Ellis, and real danger threatens. Natives surround the Club on three sides so help is not available, for the fourth side fronts on the river. Flory suddenly has "one of those startling ideas that are overlooked simply because they are so obvious . . ." (p. 249). He quickly runs to the river to swim to summon help.

> He sank deep down, and the horrible river ooze received him, sucking him knee-deep so that it was several seconds before he could free himself. When he came to the surface a tepid froth, like the froth on stout, was lapping round his lips, and some spongy thing had floated into his throat and was choking him. (p. 250)

The water is murky and dirty, in contrast to the clear, cool water of the jungle pool where Flory had retreated from the world of the Club. Here, the water is associated with the Club and its members, stagnant and vile like the water where he first encountered Elizabeth. Then and now, Flory is im-mersing himself in the water of the Club to save the Club. In the literal act of trying to protect the values which he detests and abjures he is symbolically accepting them. But those values must be maintained if he is to have their epitome, Elizabeth Lackersteen.

Ironically, Flory finds the police already roused but unable to disperse the villagers, who are like a "viscous sea" (p. 252). But finally the riot is dispelled,[11] followed by a sudden change in the climate: The monsoon season arrives and it begins raining. The regenerative rain of nature has arrived; the last alternative is present for Flory to accept. Instead, he re-enters the Club, the world of the stagnant river, through which he has just swum to maintain the extant values, but now to proceed directly to his determined fate, the fate of any deviant in the jungle populated by the Club beasts. And though Flory does not completely re-establish himself with Elizabeth until Verrall leaves town (in a train like "a black-behinded caterpillar"), he is at least able to kiss her and to be implicitly restored to favor.

He is symbolically restored to favor in the eyes of his countrymen as well. Flory tells Veraswami of his conversation with his fellow Englishmen, Ellis and Macgregor.

> "The only fly in the ointment is that I told the police to fire over the crowd's heads instead of straight at them. It seems that's against all the Government regulations. Ellis was a little vexed about it. 'Why didn't you plug some of the b—s when you had the chance?' he said. I pointed out that it would have meant hitting the police who were in the middle of the crowd; but as he said, they were only niggers anyway. However, all my sins are forgiven me. And Macgregor quoted something in Latin—Horace, I believe." (pp. 257–258)

The secular absolution by the very temporal High Priest of the Club is, of course, parody—directed both at the efficacy of organized religion[12] and at the concepts of the Club; one of the earliest descriptions of the Club is that it is "the spiritual citadel" of the town (p. 17). The metaphor is a prevision of action: just as Flory is now forgiven his sins by his heroic act of contrition, so can we anticipate his being cast to Hell. His error is in not recognizing the presence of a way to a true regeneration, the sacramental natural rain that is now an alternative: "The lovely rain streamed down, drenching him from head to foot, and filling his nostrils with the scent of earth, forgotten during the months of drought" (p. 258). Flory understands drought only as his absence from Elizabeth; in maintaining and hence accepting the values of the Club, he operates under the same misconceptions as do the other English—the real, natural world is to be avoided or, at best, tolerated; all meaning is understood in terms of social values. Or, the only jungle that has value is the one which is indoors.

Yet another beast re-enters the scene: U Po Kyin, the crocodile, who, in Veraswami's phrase, "strikes always at the weakest spot" (p. 49), does just that and involves Ma Hla May in a plot to discredit Flory—to thereby discredit Veraswami. Soon after, Flory and Elizabeth arrive at the church, where she tells him that Verrall is gone, "for good."

> There had been no need to say anymore. He had simply taken her by the arms and drawn her towards him. She came willingly, even gladly—there in the clear daylight, merciless to his disfigured face. For a moment she had clung to him almost like a child. It was as though he had saved her or protected her from something. He raised her face to kiss her, and found with surprise that she was crying. There had been no time to talk then, not even to say, "Will you marry me?" No matter, after the service there would be time enough. Perhaps at his next visit, only six weeks hence, the padre would marry them. (p. 270)

The naevus, the symbol of Flory's individuality, almost draws them together. For Elizabeth, Flory seems the only hope, and she must accept him for his naked, revealed self; in Elizabeth's favor, the tears are at least tears of gratitude if not of compassion. But there is again a crucial failure of communication; no commitment is made, the understanding is not codified by social forms. Disaster still has its opening.

Disaster arrives in the person of Ma Hla May, who at U Po Kyin's instigation abases herself in the church. She accuses Flory in front of the English, in effect violating all the social conventions of the society whose values Flory is in the process of accepting. Ma Hla May creates a terrible scene; she tears her clothes open and makes only too clear the nature of her relationship with Flory. The Club members are scandalized: "Everyone was upset by it. Even Ellis was disgusted" (p. 274). The hypocrisy is plain, and tied to the theme of the failure of language in the novel; as long as things are not said, they are all right, no matter how well-known is the wrong doing. As long as heresy is not committed to language it does not exist; conversely, for Flory, that which would have prevented all the tragedy would have been the simple articulation of betrothal. The Club world is doubly damned: It is corrupt; it corrupts language. Finally, Ma Hla May is forcibly removed.

> Flory could neither speak nor stir. He sat staring fixedly at the altar, his face rigid and so bloodless that the birthmark seemed to glow upon it like a streak of blue paint. Elizabeth glanced across the aisle at him, and her revulsion made her almost physically sick. She had not understood a word of what Ma Hla May was saying, but the meaning of the scene was perfectly clear. The thought that he had been the lover of that grey-faced, maniacal creature made her shudder in her bones. But worse than that, worse than anything, was his ugliness at this moment. His face appalled her, it was. so ghastly, rigid and old. It was like a skull. Only the birthmark seemed alive in it. She hated him now for his birthmark. She had never known till this moment how dishonouring, how unforgivable a thing it was. (p. 274)

The birthmark which had united them in an embrace, as she had come "in the clear daylight, merciless to his disfigured face . . . saved . . . protected," now separates them; the naevus becomes that which Elizabeth hates "worse than anything." The symbolic pattern is nearly completed: just as Flory rescued her, "chalk-faced," from the buffalo's horns, from a sexual threat, now at the end of the novel a horn-shape becomes again sexually defined. Flory's sexual actions with "grey-faced" Ma Hla May are more than Elizabeth and the Club can bear; they are "unforgivable."

Orwell makes the point clear: The threat is to the conventions of the Club world, through sexuality, virility, and hence individuality. Flory runs after Elizabeth, begging forgiveness, offering the denial of his own masculinity in return for mere communication.

> "Does it mean nothing to you when I say that I love you? I don't believe you've ever realised what it is that I want from you. If you like, I'd marry you and promise never even to touch you with my finger. I wouldn't mind even that, so long as you were with me. But I can't go on with my life alone, always alone. Can't you bring yourself ever to forgive me?" (p. 277)

The answer is "Never, never." Equally noteworthy is the epithet which Elizabeth has for Flory just before his final rejection. He is to her a "beast" (p. 276). The pattern is complete: As a beast at the outset brought them together, as the beast of the earthquake momentarily separated them in another crucial scene, so finally does Flory become the overt beast which again menaces her and implictly the whole system of the Club's values. And as he has earlier been accepted in religious terms by the eternal, omniscient Club, it now casts him into its outer darkness.

> She was no sooner free of him than she took to her heels and actually ran into the Club garden, so hateful was his presence to her. Among the trees she stopped to take off her spectacles and remove the signs of tears from her face. Oh, the beast, the beast! He had hurt her wrists abominably. Oh, what an unspeakable beast he was! When she thought of his face as it had looked in church, yellow and glistening with the hideous birthmark upon it, she could have wished him dead. It was not what he had done that horrified her. He might have committed a thousand abom-

inations and she could have forgiven him. But not after
that shameful, squalid scene, and the devilish ugliness of
his disfigured face in that moment. It was, finally, the
birthmark that had damned him. (p. 278)

We are aware of a final irony. Flory has become finally another beast of the Club jungle. But he has become part of
this world only to be cast out into another, real jungle.

Flory returns home and shoots first Flo and then himself.
The shot which he had earlier taken—and missed—at the
pariah dog now finds its mark. That part of Flory which was
the outcast now is formally destroyed. He shoots Flo in the
head, but seeing that "her shattered brain looked like red vel-
vet," chooses to shoot himself in "the heart, then, not the
head" (p. 281). This final gesture becomes perhaps Flory's
only triumph over those values which destroyed him. In deliberately, if unconsciously, choosing not to do what seems logical in the structure of the novel, literally destroy the cursed
birthmark, Flory manages the assertion that he had avoided
while living. The mark, which represented both his weakness
and his strength, for it was connected with both the world of
the Club and the world of the jungle, remains—and tentative
assertion of self is proclaimed.

A study of a final pattern of imagery is apposite. Throughout the novel, there are repeated references to imprisonment,
for example, numerous scenes of various natives being im-
prisoned by Westfield, the District Superintendent of Police,
scenes which seem irrelevant to the theme of the novel. Not
only do the English literally imprison the Burmese, but,
metaphorically at least, the entire novel displays the captivity
of all the characters. In their striving for English values, Burmese such as U Po Kyin and Veraswami incarcerate themselves; in the closed world of the Club, the English enslave
their servants and each other in bigotry and solipsism; perhaps most significant of all, the jungles make captives of all
inhabitants. Because they biologically share the worlds of
both Englishman and Burmese, the most captive characters

in the novel are the half-castes, Mr. Samuel and Mr. Francis. Belonging to both worlds, they are accepted by neither; and their resulting exile is a reflection of Flory's, who also tries to exist within two inimical systems of values. It is the refusal to accept the fact of environment that truly enslaves; the retreat from life-giving, regenerative nature to artificial, decaying, out-of-place systems leads the English to make a beast-filled jungle of their own lives. As spurious doubles of the natural world around them, the people of Kyauktada are like the suicide-committing insects or the lizard that stalks the moth at the moment of Flory's suicide: They kill themselves and each other. The ultimate effect of the life sentence which these people are serving is death.

That this kind of life is as meaningless as is Flory's suicide is demonstrated by the final chapter of the novel. U Po Kyin attains his dearest wish—membership in the Club—and more —a decoration from the English for his part in putting down the rebellion at the Club; he "had done all that mortal man could do" (p. 286). But before he can ensure his entrance into Nirvana by his equivalent of salvation through good works, building a pagoda, he is stricken by a heart attack and dies. And his wife suffers greatly to think of him wandering in a "dreadful subterranean hell of fire," or, worse, returning to earth "in the shape of a rat or a frog" (p. 286). The jungle is inescapable. Elizabeth inevitably marries her fellow-tortoise, Mr. Macgregor, and "fills with complete success the position for which Nature had designed her from the first, that of a burra memsahib" (p. 287). Veraswami is disgraced and demoted to exile in another hospital in Mandalay (p. 283). And John Flory is only remembered as "a dark chap with a birthmark. He shot himself in Kyauktada in 1926. Over a girl, people said. Bloody fool" (p. 283).

It is fitting that Flory's verbal epitaph should recall his birthmark, for it is this symbolic wound which finally defines the worth of Flory's life. I am thinking of Edmund Wilson's brilliant essay, "Philoctetes: The Wound and the Bow."[13] One can best understand John Flory within the framework of "the conception of superior strength as inseparable from disability." Like Philoctetes, Flory is both an outcast from his society and at the same time the only person who can save that society from perishing in the face of danger. The quality of Flory's rescue of the Club in the riot is ironic, of course, in contrast to Philoctetes' value to the Greeks. But the survival of the Club society, no matter how corrupt, does indeed depend on Flory. At the same time, like the Greeks' attitude toward Philoctetes, the people of the Club cannot tolerate the marked Flory, "who upsets the processes of normal life by his curses and his cries."[14] So society is saved; the life, normal only in its inherent horror, does become re-established; the jungle of Burma is unaffected and the jungle of the Club goes on, with its predestined sovereign, Elizabeth Lackersteen, now ruling. John Flory is remembered only for his foolishness and his birthmark.

The theme of *Burmese Days*, then, is not anticolonialism, but the failure of community—of two persons and of society. In the attempt to impose the standards and mores of a far-distant world upon an alien and unyielding landscape, the English people of Kyauktada estrange themselves from reality. They simply forget that it is Burma that is to be accommodated, not England; the implacable jungle takes its toll, alters the mode of life in accord with its own, allows the superficiality of the Club world to become only a more hidden, more savage jungle. The community is corrupted because the life is solitary and murderous, because the enforced existence in Burma becomes based on envy rather than acceptance, convention rather than love, form rather than reality.

One of the values which exists in tenuous perception in the book is the concept of communication; its failure leads to much of the tragedy of the novel. For Orwell at this point, communication is the necessary step toward and corollary of community. In *Burmese Days*, this possibility exists only as the constructive alternative, unwisely not taken. But language and its uses is to become the major concern of Orwell's career, and will come to dominate his thought and his fiction. In this first novel we see this theme present only in a context of social indignation, the corruption of language demonstrated only in the inanities of Club chatter and the inability to articulate at the crucial time.

The novel finally demands judgment on its own grounds and for its place in Orwell's career. It seems clearly enough to possess faults often found in first novels: at times it is over-written; some scenes are so melodramatic that the reader is unsure whether they are meant to be read as parody or are to be taken straight. Orwell himself seemed skeptical of the book's rhetoric when, years later, he referred to Burmese Days as an "enormous naturalistic" novel, "full of detailed descriptions and arresting similes, and also full of purple passages in which words were used partly for the sake of their sound."[15] Yet, I cannot altogether accept either his judgment or the judgments of most of his critics, who in general have little good to say for the book. The intricate symbology of the story—which I am convinced was Orwell's conscious method of unifying the novel—may well be too heavily Freudian, and thus unsatisfactory in the same way as are all psychological symbols in literature: They substitute convenience for complexity; they close rather than open meaning insofar as they categorize and limit human motive rather than allow for its ambiguity and multiplicity. But the symbols are in fact nicely incorporated into the fabric of the plot and are not as obtrusive as this necessary winnowing of them might indicate. Furthermore, they are appropriate to this fictional world. Flory's "wound," after all, is both physical and psychic, and as such it suggests both cause and result of his dilemmas: His alienation is caused by his "difference," his intellectual arrogance, in that he knows, rightly, that he is better than his fellow colonials, and as well as by his personal loneliness. The sexual aspect of such solitude is also understandable and "right" as cause and result of his alienation, his actions, and his relationship with Elizabeth. Thus, inescapably held in a situation he cannot change —nor would if he were able—he is doomed. Caught in

a jungle-world of predators, the weak, the "wounded" animal is inevitably killed; our knowledge of nature, bestial and
human, confirms this pattern. Thus, perhaps *Burmese Days*
meets the highest standard of success in art: It "reads" us,
concretizes that which we already suspect, puts in form that
which we know; *it* substantiates *us*.

The novel does not seem to possess the philosophical complexity or riches of that book with which it must be compared—*A Passage to India*. But it is necessary to keep in mind
that *Burmese Days* was Orwell's first book and *A Passage to
India* was Forster's last. Moreover, there is little evidence to
suggest that Orwell, at this point in his life anyway, shared
the boundless despair over man's inability to ever be more
than alone in this world that seems to mark Forster's novel.
Community and language fail in *Burmese Days*, but condi-
tionally; Orwell does not, I think, insist on the failure of all
communities and all relationships, at all times—as does Forster, in the terrifying and brilliant conclusion of his novel.
That the best may perish and the worst prevail is a valid
insight that Orwell insists on—but, in fairness, he suggests no
more than that. His subsequent novels indicate that Orwell
was in fact immediately dissatisfied with such an attitude as
too limiting, too restrictive. That the outcome of accepting
human society as it is will in turn be as destructive as the
loneliness Flory faced is something Orwell only later understood. At this point in his career, Orwell immediately seeks
alternatives to the pessimism and limitations that *Burmese
Days* suggests about the human spirit. For the novel, in a
profound way, portrays man as caught and injured by the best
parts of his self, destroyed by those aspects of self which
should ennoble him—love, charity, sacrifice. That such qualities are misunderstood and misused speaks more of the character of a society than of the falseness of such qualities.
Burmese Days is, despite flaws and inadequacies, a remarkable first novel. More, it reveals all of Orwell's major themes
—themes whose implications are to be extensively investi-
gated in his subsequent books. Orwell's greatest and most

far-reaching work, *1984*, will confirm the essential bases of *Burmese Days*—the terrors of Oceania will be only more efficient than those of Kyauktada; the desperation of the individual in society will be qualitatively the same.

But *Burmese Days* does not merely anticipate Orwell's long-range notions about man's relationship with the state. In a more immediate way, the implicit and explicit concerns over the frailty of human communication and the failure of language present in this novel are to become Orwell's recurring considerations. The overt subject matter of the early novels will vary widely, but the exploration of the uses and the ends of language will be consistently present. In this first novel, Orwell conceives of language only as theme. He uses the failure of language to suggest the difficulty of human communication and community; such failure comes to represent those gulfs, perhaps inevitable, between persons and between societies. Individuals speak, but their voices go unheeded. Races separate into antagonistic camps, inflamed by mindless rhetoric, sullen in their certainties of distrust and isolation. But language is merely (if such a word is acceptable in the context of human tragedy) a symbol, a metaphor—in this novel, at least. So it is both a logical step and yet an enormous leap in apprehension to Orwell's later view of language as cause as well as result, as the essence as well as the manifestation of human tyranny and suffering. It is a natural development, and yet there are the differences of a lifetime's insights between the conception of language as symbol and the portrayal of language as the means and root of that most famed and most terrifying vision of human totalitarianism in modern letters. In a precise way, Orwell's developing apprehensions about the nature of language are the touchstones necessary to understand his work. The final developments of the failure of articulation and of the example, say, of *The Burmese Patriot*, a silly nationalistic propaganda sheet, will be Newspeak, the end of human rationality and the denial of the possibility of selfhood.

II

A CLERGYMAN'S DAUGHTER

> Indeed our sweet foods leave us cavities.
> —W. D. Snodgrass, *Heart's Needle*

Within a year following the appearance of *Burmese Days*, Orwell had another book before the public. But *A Clergyman's Daughter* (1935) met with even less success than had Orwell's first novel. It is the most adversely criticized of all his books, and there is evidence that Orwell himself was dubious as to its quality. Christopher Hollis reports that Orwell refused to let the book be republished and, in fact, himself bought up and destroyed all the copies he could find.[1] Subsequent commentators on Orwell's life and work have generally shared this assessment: Frank Wadsworth finds it his "poorest novel";[2] John Atkins says it is a "hotch-potch,"[3] whatever that may be; even otherwise sympathetic Laurence Brander, though he says the book has "special interest" in being the first of Orwell's "London" novels, must call it a "failure."[4] This supposed failure is usually attributed to its so-called documentary interpolations and its episodic structure.

The book's value is commonly thought to be limited to the development of ideas and stylistic techniques initiated in *Burmese Days* and to the previsions of ideas which occur in

Orwell's subsequent writings. True, the use of animal imagery for human beings in order to suggest bestial kinds of behavior, so prominent in the structure of *Burmese Days*, is continued in *A Clergyman's Daughter*. There may be certain appropriate suggestions of timidity, of docility in the name Dorothy Hare, as well as ironic suggestions as to the nature of her sexual attitudes, for Dorothy is frigid. But it is difficult to make much of this since her father, an overbearing, officious individual, who is also completely indifferent to sex, is of course also a Hare. In a scene where Dorothy, now a teacher, is being shamefully browbeaten by a group of irate parents, one of these is called "a large, buffalo-like man."[5] The horrid Mrs. Creevy, owner of the school where Dorothy teaches for a time, is likened to a "hawk" bearing down on her students—who shrink from her like "partridge chicks" (p. 223). But there is not the patterned development of these images there was in *Burmese Days* and that there will be later. They are rather random, expressive modes of characterization. The structure of the novel is based on other matters.

There is another, more specific foreshadowing in the book. The local roué, Mr. Warburton has a favorite saying: "If you took I Corinthians, chapter thirteen, and in every verse wrote 'money' instead of 'charity,' the chapter had ten times as much meaning as before" (p. 214). This "saying" becomes the epigraph of *Keep the Aspidistra Flying*, where the problem of poverty is the main theme.

But perhaps the most significant look forward found in *A Clergyman's Daughter* is Orwell's condemnation of the newspapers, specifically *Pippin's Weekly*, "the dirtiest of the five dirty Sunday newspapers" (p. 136). In *Burmese Days*, the plot and the theme revolve around the failure of communication; at crucial times, commitment is not articulated, misunderstanding and inevitable misinterpretation arise, and tragedy follows. While misunderstanding results from the failure of communication in *A Clergyman's Daughter*, the agent, the circumstances, and the guilt are different. One bearer of guilt is *Pippin's Weekly*, the tabloid which seizes upon Dorothy's disappearance and features it repeatedly under headlines such as "PASSION DRAMA IN COUNTRY RECTORY" (p. 136). This is Orwell's first real treatment of mis-reportage in the news media. The paper, which "cared little whether its news was news so long as it was spicy," causes a scandal which in turn is partly why Reverend Hare temporarily abandons his efforts to find Dorothy. The scandal-sheet's indifference to fact anticipates the more extensive treatment of willful misrepresentation of language in Orwell's subsequent work.

This novel as well reveals an attitude which will be finally contradicted by Orwell. In many ways Orwell was the antithesis of what his admirers hold him to be: Strains of orthodoxy and conservatism often outweigh his vaunted radicalism; meanness of spirit is often apparent in the man admired for largeness of vision. His often remarked rancor toward socialists and his not-so-thinly veiled distaste for the real people whose abstract causes he championed are part of an antidemocratic strain in his writing that may be overlooked but is indisputable. *A Clergyman's Daughter* presents as its resolution a conservatism and a tolerance of the inequities and iniquities of social life that, it must be said, deny the liberal, much less radical, spirit. In fact, Orwell's resignation before tyrannies over the human mind and body—relatively minor though such despotisms are in these books—is an attitude which is present in considerable degree in his first three novels. It is reasonable to say that the one dominant resolution of these early books is the affirmation to live within the community, to accept the world as it is, to deny one's self before the demands of society. What will change is, of course, Orwell's conception of the nature of society; what will alter that conception will be primarily, as we shall see, his experiences in the Spanish Civil War and, I think, the implications of the various subjects, images, and themes he is slowly developing. At this stage in his career, however, his imagination has yet to educate his social instincts. But *A Clergyman's*

Daughter is a clear step on the road to *Animal Farm* and *1984*.

The plot of the novel is episodic. Dorothy Hare, pious, overburdened daughter of a village curate who cares more for his investments than for his parish, suddenly suffers an attack of amnesia. She wakes some days later and proceeds on a series of incredible adventures—which continue even after she has regained her memory, for her father will not take her back because of the scandal she has supposedly caused. She experiences the hop-picking world of the itinerant, the world of the down-and-out vagrant in London—including time spent in a quasi-brothel (in all innocence, of course) and in jail—and finally several months in a terrible private school before she is returned to her life at home. Each of the adventures Dorothy undergoes gives Orwell an opportunity to exploit, analyze, satirize, or castigate one or several social evils. And it is obvious that the polemicist's tone and the essayist's pose often take over. Dorothy endures the labors of hop-picking; inexperienced, she and Nobby, the man with whom she has (again innocently) joined up, can each make only about ten shillings a week.

> There were various reasons for this. To begin with, there was the badness of the hops in some of the fields. Again, there were the delays which wasted an hour or two of every day. When one plantation was finished you had to carry your bin to the next, which might be a mile distant; and then perhaps it would turn out that there was some mistake, and the set, struggling under their bins (they weighed a hundredweight), would have to waste another half hour in traipsing elsewhere. Worst of all, there was the rain. It was a bad September that year, raining one day in three. Sometimes for a whole morning or afternoon you shivered miserably in the shelter of the unstripped bines, with a dripping hop poke round your shoulders, waiting for the rain to stop. It was impossible to pick when it was raining. The hops were too slippery to handle, and if you did pick them it was worse than useless, for when sodden with

water they shrank all to nothing in the bin. Sometimes
you were in the fields all day to earn a shilling or less.
(pp. 130–131)

The information sounds right (one often senses Orwell's own
experiences back of those of his characters), and it explains
why Dorothy cannot earn enough money on which to live.
But, in fact, the passage loses sight of Dorothy; Orwell seems
more interested in the mechanics of hop-picking. The passage
has no real function within the plot; it retards the action
rather than helps it, for what interests the reader is how Dorothy is affected by this manner of life, not the effect of water
on hops. But Orwell goes on, in just this vein, for several
more paragraphs. And though passages of this kind are relatively infrequent in the novel, there are enough to justify
attributions of "documentary" to the various episodes of
Dorothy's journey.

Such passages spoil the conventional unity and justify the
designation episodic. But this need not be pejorative. If we
think of this novel as picaresque, the seemingly random
adventures the protagonist experiences must conventionally
be disparate, revealing varied inequities in the society which
is explored. So considered, the book maintains several ironies:
Unlike the conventional *picaro*, Dorothy is neither roguish
nor clever. She is innocent in the extreme—sexually frigid,
socially ignorant, intellectually empty. When she first arrives
in London, she is unable to find a room, since a "single girl
with no luggage is invariably a bad lot—this is the first and
greatest of the apophthegms of the London landlady" (p.
157). She finally finds a room at "Mary's" and goes apprehen-
sively to bed.

The walls were so thin that you could hear everything that
was happening. There were bursts of shrill idiotic laughter,
hoarse male voices singing, a gramophone drawling out
limericks, noisy kisses, strange deathlike groans, and once
or twice the violent rattling of an iron bed. Towards mid-
night the noises began to form themselves into a rhythm

in Dorothy's brain, and she fell lightly and unrestfully
asleep. She was woken about a minute later, as it seemed,
by her door being flung open, and two dimly-seen female
shapes rushed in, tore every scrap of clothing from her bed
except the sheets, and rushed out again. There was a
chronic shortage of blankets at "Mary's," and the only way
of getting enough of them was to rob somebody else's
bed. (pp. 160–161)

Almost unbelievably, it takes Dorothy nearly a week to come
to understand what Mary's is—not actually a brothel, but a
"refuge of prostitutes" (p. 164). But it is really not so unbe-
lievable that Dorothy should fail to understand this, for life
in Knype Hill, her home, has given her no inkling of the
existence of such a world. Perhaps the apparent strainings
of credibility in this book are dramatically consistent and
believable.

The cause of Dorothy's adventures is, of course, her amnesia attack. But this too has been criticized as being illogical:
". . . for no very clear reason—but doubtless aphasia comes
like that—she loses her memory and runs away."[6] This is
simply not the case, and such criticism demonstrates an un-
willingness to examine Orwell's writing on *his* terms. Just
prior to her loss of memory Dorothy has suffered one indignity after another. It is stressed that she has worked herself
to the point of exhaustion in carrying out what should be
her father's duties in his church. She has had to attempt,
unsuccessfully, to get more money from her father to pay the
ever pressing creditors with whom she must deal. She must
shift from market to market in order to maintain credit.
Finally, she is lured into Warburton's home under a false
pretext, and he makes a typically ineffectual, but nevertheless unnerving, assault. In sum, in the day that precedes
Dorothy's loss of memory, she has very "clear reason" for becoming ill. And the trials of this day are at the thematic core
of the novel. Being subjected in her own way to the pressures
of organized religion, poverty, education, sex, and overwhelming work, Dorothy breaks down. The experiences which she

then undergoes as a result of this breakdown recapitulate these trials in a larger social world. Moreover, the results of the amnesia are an enlargement of the cause; Dorothy's private tribulations are symbolic of the problems of the public world. At the end of the novel, we can expect that Dorothy's personal solution to her problems will be Orwell's suggested resolution for such public concerns.

The first true cause of Dorothy's amnesia is the monstrosity of organized religion. Orwell expresses his attack primarily by the characterization of two persons: pastor and parishioner, Mr. Hare and Mrs. Pither. Reverend Hare is portrayed mercilessly, in a tone if not in a rhetoric which suggests Miltonic indignation at the corrupt clergy. He has a mid-Victorian attitude toward townspeople and parishioners, a mixture of *noblesse oblige* and social Darwinism. The merchants "expect to be kept waiting for their money." A grocer's request for payment is "the kind of thing that we are exposed to in this delightful century. That is democracy—progress, as they are pleased to call it. Don't order from the fellow again. Tell him at once that you are taking your account elsewhere" (p. 32). Yet if this were the extent of Rector Hare's irresponsibility, the characterization would be primarily humorous, a simple parody of the stuffy country rector. His concern with "Sumatra Tin shares" instead of the pressing domestic burdens would be pompous and somewhat irresponsible—but neither malevolent nor critical. But Orwell makes him a more evil character. At breakfast, the Rector is told of a crisis in one of his parish families. A baby is dying and the Rector is asked to come and baptize the child, who is "turning quite black."

> The Rector emptied his mouth with an effort. "Must I have these disgusting details while I am eating my breakfast?" he exclaimed. He turned on Ellen: "Send Porter about his business and tell him I'll be round at his house at twelve o'clock. I really cannot think why it is that the lower classes always seem to choose mealtimes to come

pestering one," he added, casting another irritated glance at Dorothy as she sat down. (p. 29)

Indifferent to his position and to the moral demands of Christian beliefs, Reverend Hare reveals another sin which condemns him. When Dorothy later regains her memory, she writes her father about what has happened and asks for help. He does not respond, and without his help she proceeds further down the ladder of the sub-worlds into which she has descended. Only later do we learn the reason for his not responding directly to save her. The morning Dorothy disappears, the Rector, already indignant at having to heat his own shaving water, must undergo what is for him a monstrous ordeal:

> . . . there occurred a frightful, unprecedented thing—a thing—a thing never to be forgotten this side of the grave; the Rector was obliged to prepare his own breakfast—yes, actually to mess about with a vulgar black kettle and rashers of Danish Bacon—with his own sacerdotal hands.
>
> After that, of course, his heart was hardened against Dorothy forever. (pp. 204–205)

Orwell's irony is overt and scathing. Rector Hare's solipsism, his callous indifference about his parishioners, his total lack of concern for his own daughter—all these reveal him to be enough in himself to drive a person to mental breakdown.

But the religious attitude of Rector Hare is not the sole target of Orwell's invective. The religious attitudes of the parishioners receive comparable condemnation, in language, however, that is more subtle than that reserved for Reverend Hare. Mrs. Pither and her husband, both over seventy, are "one of the few genuinely pious couples" that Dorothy visits on her rounds when she substitutes for her absentee father. But the piety of this couple demonstrates everything that Orwell felt was wrong with religion. Continually recalling her miseries, Mrs. Pither can look forward only to the next life. This life is a series of pains, never to be assuaged "in this

world," but the mention of "Heaven" brings a mystical transformation in Mrs. Pither.

> "Ah, Miss, there you said it! That's a true word, Miss!
> That's what Pither and me keeps a-saying to ourselves.
> And that's just the one thing as keeps us a-going—just the
> thought of Heaven and the long, long rest we'll have there.
> Whatever we've suffered, we gets it all back in Heaven,
> don't we, Miss? Every little bit of suffering you gets it back
> a hundredfold and a thousandfold. That is true, ain't it,
> Miss? There's rest for us all in Heaven—rest and peace and
> no more rheumatism nor digging nor cooking nor launder-
> ing nor nothing. You do believe that, don't you, Miss
> Dorothy?" (pp. 60–61)

According to Mrs. Pither, Heaven is the place where avarice
and greed are acceptable: Mrs. Pither, after all, wants her
suffering paid off in pleasure multiplied by the thousands.
But the truly grievous "sin" here is the implied lack of concern for the amelioration of social ills in the temporal world.
Orwell states this belief precisely in a later essay when he
contrasts the humanist and the Christian attitudes toward
existence.

> Most people get a fair amount of fun out of their lives,
> but on balance life is suffering, and only the very young
> or the very foolish imagine otherwise. Ultimately it is the
> Christian attitude which is self-interested and hedonistic,
> since the aim is always to get away from the painful
> struggle of earthly life and find eternal peace in some kind
> of Heaven or Nirvana. The humanist attitude is that the
> struggle must continue and that death is the price of life.
> "Men must endure their going hence, even as their com-
> ing hither: Ripeness is all"—which is an un-Christian senti-
> ment. Often there is a seeming truce between the humanist
> and the religious believer, but in fact their attitudes can-
> not be reconciled: one must choose between this world
> and the next.[7]

The full significance of the attitude which Mrs. Pither—and
by implication, in Orwell's own term, the "religious believer"

—holds is this: To live amid this world's problems but assume that solutions are possible only in another world is to deny the meaning of existence. Exact solutions, temporary or permanent, may indeed be impossible. But that is no justification for not attempting to do *something*. Dorothy's attitude at the outset of the novel is that of the religious believer —as we shall see, the hyper-penitential believer. At the end of the novel, she will have come to a new understanding of her beliefs; she will, in short, move much closer to the position of the humanist that Orwell describes.

The "satire" of religion has, then, a thematic function in the novel; it also works in the plot as a believable cause of Dorothy's amnesia. The quality of Dorothy's faith is depicted in terms which suggest inevitable waning: her faith is ever present, but only because she continually mortifies herself to keep from lapsing. She rises on the fateful morning, tired, "aching from head to foot," but she prepares to take a cold bath: "Her body had gone goose-flesh all over. She detested cold baths; it was for that very reason that she made it a rule to take all her baths cold from April to November" (p. 6). A clearer symbol of the continual self-mortification which she undergoes to keep her religion uncontaminated is the pin with which she continually pricks herself.

> Dorothy drew a long glass-headed pin from the lapel of her coat, and furtively, under cover of Miss Mayfill's back, pressed the point against her forearm. Her flesh tingled apprehensively. She made it a rule, whenever she caught herself not attending to her prayers, to prick her arm hard enough to make blood come. It was her chosen form of self-discipline, her guard against irreverence and sacrilegious thoughts. (pp. 12–13)

But even continuing self-mutilation cannot maintain faith in the face of the harsh realities of existence. Moments after pricking herself because of her wandering devotion, Dorothy suffers a "deadly blasphemy": She does not wish to drink from the communion cup after Miss Mayfill, whose lip, "pen-

dulous with age, slobbered forward, exposing a strip of gum
and row of false teeth as yellow as the keys of an old piano.
Suddenly, spontaneously, as though the Devil himself had
put it there, the prayer slipped from Dorothy's lips: 'O God,
let me not have to take the chalice after Miss Mayfill!' "
(p. 14). Dorothy immediately sticks herself, so hard that she
can scarcely suppress a cry of pain; even this is not enough
to still the natural, human loathing she feels. She is about
to step down from the altar rather than drink with such a
corrupted heart.

> Then it happened that she glanced sidelong, through the
> open south door. A momentary spear of sunlight had
> pierced the clouds. It struck downwards through the leaves
> of the limes, and a spray of leaves in the doorway gleamed
> with a transient, matchless green, greener than jade or
> emerald or Atlantic waters. It was as though some jewel of
> unimaginable splendour had flashed for an instant, filling
> the doorway with green light, and then faded. A flood of
> joy ran through Dorothy's heart. The flash of living colour
> had brought back to her, by a process deeper than reason,
> her peace of mind, her love of God, her power of worship.
> Somehow, because of the greenness of the leaves, it was
> again possible to pray. O all ye green things upon the
> earth, praise ye the Lord! She began to pray, ardently,
> joyfully, thankfully. The wafer melted upon her tongue.
> (pp. 15–16)

This momentary acceptance of a green world full of natural
joy introduces another of the motifs of the opening section,
one which is carried through to the end of the novel—Dorothy's pantheistic feelings. In another scene, when she is leaving the Pithers' house deadly tired, depressed after giving
Mrs. Pither a massage in a room smelling of urine and pare-
goric, Dorothy begins to cycle home when she spies a wild
rose and stops along side of the road to pick it. She is almost
overwhelmed.

> Her heart swelled with sudden joy. It was that mystical
> joy in the beauty of the earth and the very nature of things

that she recognised, perhaps mistakenly, as the love of God. As she knelt there in the heat, the sweet odour and the drowsy hum of insects, it seemed to her that she could momentarily hear the mighty anthem of praise that the earth and all created things send up everlastingly to their maker. All vegetation, leaves, flowers, grass, shining, vibrating, crying out in their joy. Larks also chanting, choirs of larks, invisible, dripping music from the sky. All the riches of summer, the warmth of the earth, the song of birds, the fume of cows, the droning of countless bees, mingling and ascending like the smoke of ever-burning altars. Therefore with Angels and Archangels! She began to pray, and for a moment she prayed ardently, blissfully, forgetting herself in the joy of her worship. Then, less than a minute later, she discovered that she was kissing the frond of the fennel that was still against her face. (pp. 64–65)

But Dorothy suddenly becomes aware of the falseness of this nature-worship, this "half-pagan ecstasy." She takes a thorn from a wild rose and pricks "her arm three times, to remind herself of the Three Persons of the Trinity." It seems as if any convenient artifact will serve penitential masochism.

The reader's first impulse is to see in the spontaneous, uncorrupted pantheism of this incident a religion more meaningful than the Anglicanism of the pious Mrs. Pither whom Dorothy had just left.[8] In contrast with the corrupt and corrupting organized religion that has been portrayed up to this point, the religion of nature indeed seems a more complete, more valid form of belief than does a religion which demands continued self-mortification and abasement. But in the terms of Dorothy's own search and the novel's primary theme, the pantheism suggested here is a false resolution. For it too is misdirected: It does not minister to the real world. If nature-worship does suggest that the physical world at least has some relation to the problem of faith, this kind of worship still ignores too much of the real, social world; it too is an evasion —no matter how comfortingly portrayed. At the end of the novel, still strying to find some coherent whole in which to have faith, Dorothy rejects that "pantheistic cheer-up stuff" (p. 316).

The veiled implications of masochism in Dorothy's self-mortification suggest another cause for her sudden loss of memory—her sexual aberration. As Dorothy responds to the warmth of some parts of nature, so is she repelled by the natural sexual instinct. Mr. Warburton, her pursuer, is certainly neither admirable nor attractive, but Orwell makes clear that it is the fact of sex that repels Dorothy, not the particular male. Warburton lures her to his house and is rather indifferently trying to seduce her, acting more as if it were a role the village cad must perform than as if he really expected or wanted success.

> Dorothy caught sight of the hand that was caressing her— a large, pink, very masculine hand, with thick fingers and a fleece of gold hairs upon the back. She turned very pale; the expression of her face altered from mere annoyance to aversion and dread. (p. 88)

Dorothy responds to sex consistently in this manner—characterizing it as "all that." At the end of the novel, when Warburton appears once more, a bald, panting *deus ex machina* to rescue her from Mrs. Creevy's school, he again attempts to seduce her in the railroad compartment on the way home —this time with warnings of her future barren life but with the added (but dishonest) promise of marriage.

> Mr. Warburton tightened his grip and pulled her against him. It broke the spell. The visions that had held her helpless—visions of poverty and of escape from poverty— suddenly vanished and left only a shocked realisation of what was happening to her. She was in the arms of a man —a fattish, oldish man! A wave of disgust and deadly fear went through her, and her entrails seemed to shrink and freeze. His thick male body was pressing her backwards and downwards, his large, pink face, smooth, but to her eyes old, was bearing down upon her own. The harsh odour of maleness forced itself into her nostrils. She recoiled. Furry

thighs of satyrs! She began to struggle furiously, though indeed he made hardly any effort to retain her, and in a moment she had wrenched herself free and fallen back into her seat, white and trembling. (pp. 305–306)

The fault is clearly Dorothy's. Warburton is dishonest and amoral, but the distortion of reality is Dorothy's. He is "fattish, oldish," but her first repulsion is that she is in the arms of "a man"—that is, any man. "To her eyes old" is to our eyes human; the "furry thighs of satyrs" is an exaggeration of normal human sensuality, the continuation of her aversion to the hair on his arm when he first attempted to seduce her. A conventional symbol for human potency and sexuality, hair is repulsive to Dorothy. Interestingly, at the outset of the story, Dorothy's hair is described as "thick, fine, exceedingly pale," "her only positive beauty," which her father has forbidden that she cut (p. 8). Her father, who is dramatically responsible for Dorothy's sexual frustration, assumes symbolic responsibility as well. He forces her to work so much and so hard that she is unable even to contemplate marriage and thus live a normal (i.e., sexually fulfilled) life. At the same time, he demands that the appearance of sexual vitality be maintained. Dorothy's life is little more than a series of frustrations and irreconcilable tensions.

In what is, however, an unnecessary further explanation of the cause of Dorothy's frigidity, Orwell spells out, over simply I suggest, the original source of Dorothy's attitudes.

> . . . though her sexual coldness seemed to her natural and inevitable, she knew well enough how it was that it had begun. She could remember, as clearly as though it were yesterday, certain dreadful scenes between her father and her mother—scenes that she had witnessed when she was no more than nine years old. They had left a deep, secret wound in her mind. And then a little later she had been frightened by some old steel engravings of nymphs pursued by satyrs. To her childish mind there was something inexplicably, horribly sinister in those horned, semi-human creatures that lurked in thickets and behind large trees,

ready to come bounding forth in sudden swift pursuit. For a whole year of her childhood she had actually been afraid to walk through woods alone, for fear of satyrs. She had grown out of the fear, of course, but not out of the feeling that was associated with it. The satyr had remained with her as a symbol. Perhaps she would never grow out of it, that special feeling of dread, of hopeless flight from something more than rationally dreadful—the stamp of hooves in the lonely wood, the lean, furry thighs of the satyr. It was a thing not to be altered, not to be argued away. It is, moreover, a thing too common nowadays, among educated women, to occasion any kind of surprise. (pp. 93–94)

The cause smacks of cocktail-party Freudianism, stereotyped pictures of the innocent child forever marred by some unspeakable, no matter how normal, accidental introduction to sex. And even more indicative of Orwell's mishandling of Dorothy's frigidity is the moralistic tone of the last sentence, with the sneer at education bursting through. The fact of the matter is that it does seem as if Dorothy's frigidity is supererogatory. Her pursuit by Warburton could be as meaningful a cause of her subsequent dilemma without the complication of abnormality; in fact, if her aversion were to him rather than in herself, it would add to the pressures which so suddenly bear upon her.

For it is made clear by Orwell that the primary cause of Dorothy's sudden attack is simple human fatigue. And the primary cause of her amnesia, work, becomes at the end of the book the solution—such as it is—to the problems of her existence, and to the problems of social life posited by Orwell. In effect, the disease becomes the cure.

The day prior to her attack of amnesia Dorothy rises early to feed her father, passes a full morning of domestic chores, worrying about the local merchants; she must also attend to nearly all the duties of the parish, and make costumes for a forthcoming children's pageant (a scene which anticipates Dorothy's later involvement with schoolchildren at Mrs. Creevy's). The afternoon is no less overwhelming.

> She had had an exhausting afternoon, starting off with ten
> miles or so of bicycling to and fro in the sun, delivering
> the parish magazine, and continuing with the Mothers'
> Union tea in the hot little wooden-walled room behind the
> parish hall. . . . After tea Dorothy had dashed up to the
> church to put fresh flowers on the altar, and then she had
> typed out her father's sermon—her typewriter was a rickety
> pre-Boer War "invisible," on which you couldn't average
> eight hundred words an hour—and after supper she had
> weeded the pea rows until the light failed and her back
> seemed to be breaking. With one thing and another, she
> was even more tired than usual. (pp. 85–86)

But Dorothy could not yet go home; she returned to the Rectory to finish making the costumes for the pageant, "dreadfully, overwhelmingly tired." But there is work to be done.

> . . . there was a somehow exceptional quality about her
> tiredness to-night. She felt, in an almost literal sense of
> the words, washed out. As she stood beside the table she
> had a sudden, very strange feeling as though her mind had
> been entirely emptied, so that for several seconds she
> actually forgot what it was that she had come into the
> conservatory to do. (p. 95)

The passage obviously foreshadows Dorothy's forthcoming
loss of memory and should be noted by those who claim the
amnesia unmotivated. More important, the scene unmistakably designates work as the primary cause of her loss of memory and thus of her subsequent adventures. The other problems which Dorothy has faced during her day have been
many—inadequate funds; the pressures of a tenuously maintained religion; the difficulties of controlling restive, mis-
chievous children; finally, the indignities of sexual frustration.
But all these are subsumed into the purview of work, of a
fatigue which "mechanically" overwhelms her, as she sits
pasting costumes and "pinching herself every two minutes to
counteract the hypnotic sound of the oilstove singing beneath
the glue pot" (p. 95).

I make much of the opening section (roughly a third of the book) and for two reasons pass somewhat swiftly over the particular adventures that Dorothy undergoes after she wakes up in her new surroundings the next morning. Most attention devoted to A *Clergyman's Daughter* has been directed to the middle section of the novel, looking at the three separate adventures Dorothy passes through—and generally looking at these so-called "documentaries" for what they reveal about Orwell's attitudes toward life in the hop-fields, life down and out in London, and life in a public school. When attention is thus focused, the inevitable result has been a failure to consider the book as a novel. But the entire structure and the major theme of the book are dependent upon the opening section, in which all the necessary motivation is given for Dorothy's amnesia and which, in fact, anticipates precisely Dorothy's peregrinations. That is, the middle of the book only develops in detail those elements in Dorothy's life which have caused her to be taken away from her former environment.

The first of the adventures, the experience with the hop-pickers, is an intensification of Dorothy's money-worries and her labor in Knype Hill. Ironically, in this world those elements which so pressed upon Dorothy at home also exist, but here they are assimilated into an appropriate frame of reference and thus are "acceptable"—a word important in the climax of the book. Nobby, Dorothy's companion, tried "to make love to Dorothy, of course," but when she repulses him, he bears her no grudge and they remain companions (p. 112). Even hard, physical labor, which caused her illness, does not trouble Dorothy in this context, where it is appropriate and "customary": "It was stupid work, mechanical, exhausting and every day more painful to the hands," "yet you were happy with an unreasonable happiness. The work took hold of you and absorbed you" (p. 127). In the end picking hops is useful, while drinking tea with pious parishioners is not; to Orwell useful work, however painful, is an acceptable occupation. The distinction lies in the effect of the work, here as normal as are the sexual advances. Here, in this sub-world, sex is treated as a natural part of a human condition ("of course" Nobby tried to make love to Dorothy); when Dorothy repulses him, for whatever private reason she has, this too is natural. Likewise, work is natural. It may be stupid and blind; the hop-pickers are oppressed and exploited—and Orwell interpolates social criticism to make this clear—but the work they perform at least has a useful purpose. The world may be, on balance, wrong and repressive, but it is accepted as existent, and the people within the confines of the world make the best possible adjustment. The attitude is typically Orwellian: Better to struggle within a wrong society than to attempt, *hopelessly*, to reform the society from without. Mr. Warburton later tells Dorothy that the world she inhabits is pointless, personally, spiritually, and socially, and he offers her (falsely, as a matter of fact) an alternative, an escape. At the end, Dorothy cannot accept such evasion.

The second episode into which Dorothy's amnesia leads her (she has by now regained her memory, but because of her father's "position" she cannot return home) is the Trafalgar Square scene, the epitome of Dorothy's time "down and out" in London. Finally forced to leave Mary's when her scant money is gone, Dorothy arrives, "by the process of gravitation that draws all roofless people to the same spot, at Trafalgar Square" (p. 166). Dorothy's night in Trafalgar Square is Orwell's only technical experimentation in his writings. In its use of the stream-of-consciousness and surrealism, the scene is reminiscent of the Circe episode in Joyce's *Ulysses*.[9] In the drama, which well suggests the chaos of a night in the square, the various elements of Dorothy's prior life appear and disappear. A character who also spends the night on the park benches is Mr. Tallboys, one-time Rector of "Little Fawley-cum-Dewsbury." If there were any doubt, even after his characterization of Reverend Hare, about Orwell's attitude toward the clergy qua clergy, the portrait of

Mr. Tallboys would erase it. He moves from revelations of banal cliches, intermixed with admissions of corruption:

> "Happy days, happy days! My ivied church under the sheltering hillside—my red-tiled Rectory slumbering among Elizabethan yews! My library, my vinery, my cook, house-parlourmaid and groom-gardener! My cash in the bank, my name in Crockford! My black suit of irreproachable cut, my collar back to front, my watered silk cassock in the church precincts. . . ." (p. 168)

through admissions of perversion:

> "My curate days, my curate days! My fancywork bazaars and morris dances in aid of the village green, my lectures to the Mothers' Union—missionary work in Western China with fourteen magic lantern slides! My Boys' Cricket Club, teetotallers only, my confirmation classes— purity lecture once monthly in the Parish Hall—my Boy Scout orgies! The Wolf Cubs will deliver the Grand Howl. Household Hints for the Parish Magazine, 'Discarded Fountainpen fillers can be used as enemas for canaries. . . .' " (pp. 181–182)

to a final, parodic picture of the clergyman as Prince of Hell:

> "Maledicite, omnia opera! The Black Mass! Why not? Once a priest always a priest. Hand me a chunk of toke and I will work the miracle. Sulphur candles, Lord's Prayer backwards, crucifix upside down. (To Dorothy) If we had a black he-goat you would come in useful." (p. 191)

Intermixed with formal religion are the other elements which Dorothy has experienced: poverty, ignorance, hunger. Despite the unconventional form of the scene, the impression is that of a realistic, terrible night spent as a vagrant in London. Into this kind of life, of necessity, Dorothy becomes hardened.

So she stayed in London, and became one of that curious

tribe, rare but never quite extinct—the tribe of women who are penniless and homeless, but who make such desperate efforts to hide it that they very nearly succeed; women who wash their faces at drinking fountains in the cold of the dawn, and carefully uncrumple their clothes after sleepless nights, and carry themselves with an air of reserve and decency, so that only their faces, pale beneath sunburn, tell you for certain that they are destitute. (p. 201)

Finally arrested, after begging from a "nasty old lady with a face like a horse," Dorothy spends a night in jail. She is rescued from this life by her uncle, who has been asked to intercede by Dorothy's father, typically still unwilling to become involved himself. Sir Thomas Hare, whose "chief characteristic was an abysmal mental vagueness" (p. 207), is himself not eager to help Dorothy, but in an attempt to still the scandal that *Pippin's Weekly* intermittently recalls about the family name he does arrange for Dorothy to teach at "Ringwood House Academy for Girls," a private school in Southbridge, a "repellent suburb" about ten miles from London.[10] This is the scene of the last of Dorothy's adventures.

Orwell's target now moves from religion and social injustice to education—or at least to certain aspects of the school world. Mrs. Creevy, the incredibly venal, callous woman who owns the school, who nearly starves Dorothy as much out of meanness as penury, lectures her on the purpose of education:

"What you've got to get hold of once and for all," she began, "is that there's only one thing that matters in a school, and that's the fees. As for all this stuff about 'developing the children's minds,' as you call it, it's neither here nor there. It's the fees I'm after, not *developing the children's minds*. After all, it's no more than common sense. It's not to be supposed as anyone'd go to all the trouble of keeping school and having the house turned upside down by a pack of brats, if it wasn't that there's a bit of money to be made out of it. The fees come first, and everything else comes afterwards." (p. 255)

Dorothy does not believe this, of course, and does not adhere to it. In spite of all the obstacles that Mrs. Creevy throws up, Dorothy actually becomes a good teacher who stimulates the children out of their fear and lethargy. She spends her own small salary to buy new texts, gets the children involved in map-making rather than the rote memorization of the capitals of the world—in short, introduces them to their own minds.

"But of course, it could not last" (p. 245). When Dorothy teaches *Macbeth*, she explains the meaning of Macduff's being "from his mother's womb/Untimely ripp'd." The children, excited and interested, bring the tale home, and the parents rise against Dorothy. It is more than their charges of indecency, however, that Orwell indicts; it is an entire concept of education, exemplified by one of the parents: "We don't send our children to school to have ideas put into their heads. . . . Practical work—that's what we want—practical work! Not all this messy stuff like po'try and making maps and sticking scraps on paper and such like. Give 'em a good bit of figuring and handwriting and bother the rest. Practical work!" (pp. 251–252). If Mrs. Creevy is antieducational in her blatant greed, so are the parents in their mania for the "practical." A system of education and an attitude toward it are on trial—not merely the corrupt few schools such as Ringwood. This attitude is parallel to Orwell's feelings about organized religion: Fairly or not, the individual evil is meant to stand for the total system.

It is not her run-in with the parents that causes Dorothy to lose her job eventually. Mrs. Creevy would not fire a person merely for the violation of principle; she rather forces Dorothy to teach the students in the manner they were previously taught. Dorothy is only fired at the close of the term —when Mrs. Creevy finds another teacher in a similar school who will pirate some of her pupils away to Ringwood in return for a percentage of their fees. Dorothy is once again cast out on the street, apparently to resume her wanderings.

At this point Mr. Warburton magically reappears, with

news that the scandal has been ended in Knype Hill (Mrs. Semprill, the gossip, has been discredited in a *different* scandal), and he brings Dorothy back, with the one more attempt at seduction, to her home. Superficially, the novel has only come full circle. Dorothy returns to her father, to her church and her religion, to the same life she led before her attack of amnesia. But there has been one major change: Dorothy has lost her faith—and this implies much. It forces, above all, her search for a new life. In the train Warburton ridicules Dorothy's religious attitudes, not understanding when she tells him that things have changed and that she is not going back to the same old life as he charges she will: ". . . if my faith is gone, what does it matter whether I've only lost it now or whether I'd really lost it years ago? All that matters is that it's gone, and I've got to begin my life over again. . . . The point is that all the beliefs I had are gone, and I've nothing to put in their place" (pp. 296–297).

The final scene of the novel provides that which is to take the place of faith. Dorothy returns to her former way of life, returns, in fact, to making costumes for the St. George's Day pageant. As Dorothy sits, pasting and cutting, she expresses the problems she faces in language that would have been out of character at the outset of the novel but which is now completely credible with her background of experience: ". . . it was the deadly emptiness that she had discovered at the heart of things. . . . Faith vanishes, but the need for faith remains the same as before" (p. 315). Now accepting a temporal world as final, for "something had happened in her heart" (p. 294), Dorothy searches for something, "some purpose in the world which you can serve, and which, while serving it, you can understand" (p. 315).

> Her mind struggled with the problem while perceiving that there was no solution. There was, she saw clearly, no possible substitute for faith; no pagan acceptance of life as sufficient to itself, no pantheistic cheer-up stuff, no pseudo-religion of "progress" with visions of glittering Utopiæ and ant-heaps of steel and concrete. It is all or

nothing. Either life on earth is a preparation for something greater and more lasting, or it is meaningless, dark and dreadful.[11]

Then Dorothy is described as being startled by a "frizzling sound" coming from the glue-pot. The glue-pot over which Dorothy labored in deep fatigue on the night she vanished from Knype Hill seems to signal that Dorothy has returned to the same onerous labor as she left, that she has found no change beyond a new awareness that life, "if the grave really ends it, is monstrous and dreadful" (p. 312). In her despair, Dorothy prays, "Lord, I believe, help Thou my unbelief. Lord, I believe, I believe; help Thou my unbelief." But, it is "useless, absolutely useless." However, once again there comes "into her nostrils a warm, evil smell, forgotten these eight months but unutterably familiar—the smell of glue" (p. 318).

> The smell of glue was the answer to her prayer. She did not know this. She did not reflect, consciously, that the solution to her difficulty lay in accepting the fact that there was no solution; that if one gets on with the job that lies to hand, the ultimate purpose of the job fades into insignificance; that faith and no faith are very much the same provided that one is doing what is customary, useful and acceptable. She could not formulate these thoughts as yet, she could only live them. Much later, perhaps, she would formulate them and draw comfort from them. (pp. 318–319)

This answer has been implicit throughout the novel. Dorothy's life in Knype Hill was desperate and degrading, but in contrast to the evasiveness of her father and of Mrs. Pither, who live for other, unreal values or in terms of another, unreal world, her life had meaning. The labor of the hop-picking provided value in itself, no matter the social indignities it presumed: It gave "a physical joy, a warm satisfied feeling inside you" (p. 127). The teaching of the school-children at Mrs. Creevy's was ineluctably doomed to failure, for numerous reasons; Dorothy's position there was "virtually that of a slave; but that did not greatly worry her. Her work was too absorbing, too all-important. In comparison with it, her own comfort and even her future hardly seemed to matter" (p. 237). At the best, there may eventually be ameliorative or beneficial results from work: The hop-pickers' conditions may be improved; some child may have been helped in some way which only the future will prove. But even at the worst, work is more valuable than ineffectual lamentation or evasion. To hope for reward in the next world is to abandon this world; to spend one's life in the pursuit of pleasure, as does Warburton, is an empty hedonism that kills the senses, ironically, "by overwork in a lifetime of squalid affairs with women" (p. 307). The book posits acceptance: Different worlds exist; different demands are made.[12] Dorothy's behavior in the malevolent world of 1984 would be cowardice; in the empty world of Knype Hill, her acceptance of limitations is courage.[13]

But if this is the final theme of the book, one must express reservations. "Doing what is customary, useful and acceptable" suggests an orthodoxy and passivity which fails to make needed distinctions. What is customary in a totalitarian world is obedience; what is useful in a corrupt society is indifference; what is acceptable in the world of Oceania is, we shall see, "unconsciousness." I do not wish to adopt the attitude Christopher Hollis so often expresses in his reservations regarding the "fairness" of the pictures of the various social forms Orwell portrays. I am willing to accept, on Orwell's own terms, his pictures of rectory life or the advertising business, pictures Hollis feels compelled to criticize as unfair and unbalanced.[14] But one must point out as an inconsistency in a man apotheosized as a social saint an attitude which assigns an individual's fate not to the determination of any standard of right or wrong, but rather to any status quo which may exist. Dorothy Hare's life around a glue-pot devoted to the "useful" may indeed some day find meaning and have great effect in Knype Hill. But such a life is, after all, only a confirmation of the attitudes of the parents of the children of Mrs.

Creevy's school in their insistence upon what is "practical."
And the acceptance of what is "useful" will become an unten-
able attitude for a writer who is to explore a spectrum of
tyrannies over man. Orwell's development, however, is gradual. The problem of a "useful" life is very much the subject
of his next novel, *Keep the Aspidistra Flying.*

III

KEEP THE
ASPIDISTRA FLYING

> To know
> That which before us lies in daily life
> Is the prime Wisdom; what is more, is fume,
> Or emptiness, or fond impertinence
> And renders us in things that most concern
> Unpractic'd, unprepar'd, and still to seek.
> —*Paradise Lost*

In *A Clergyman's Daughter*, we noted a "favorite saying" of Warburton in which he substitutes "money" for "charity" in I Corinthians 13. This parody becomes the epigraph of *Keep the Aspidistra Flying*, and its use here suggests that in the course of writing *A Clergyman's Daughter* Orwell had discovered the theme of his next novel. In the latter, one of the several facts of modern life which oppressed Dorothy Hare was the lack of money. *Keep the Aspidistra Flying* (1936), Orwell's third novel in three years and fourth book in four, has as its central theme, in its protagonist's words, "the struggle against the money-god."

Because Gordon Comstock's own struggle against the "money-god" is so closely related to the theme of the novel and because his character is so dominant in the action of the plot, criticism of this book has consistently focused on his character. Unfortunately, the tendency is to associate Comstock and Orwell. For Christopher Hollis, "Comstock is Orwell with all the fun left out."[1] Laurence Brander makes a more detailed comparison.

Gordon was middle class, educated, well read and tries to write. He can be witty, as Orwell can, understanding as Orwell can, sudden and quick in thought, as Orwell was . . . when he is socially submerged, as Orwell once was, we can believe that his mind suffers as Orwell's did. It shows how easy it is to identify Orwell with his creations.[2]

The identification of Orwell and his characters which runs through all criticism of his writing is to a degree justifiable, for the biographical basis of at least his early books is undeniable. In this instance, we know that Orwell himself spent time working in a cheap London bookstore as does Gordon Comstock. John Mander, for example, says that Gordon's "snarling at the 'nancy-boys' who frequent the bookshop where he is working" . . . is an "obsession" that is "clearly not Gordon Comstock's, but Orwell's."[3] It *is clearly* Comstock's; whether or not it is Orwell's is far less clear, less certain, and, above all, less relevant.

A better approach than biographical criticism is to see Gordon as a logical continuation of John Flory and Dorothy Hare. Like Flory, Gordon is disenfranchised from the norm of his society; unlike Flory, however, Gordon has chosen his isolation. Like Dorothy, Gordon experiences the sub-worlds of England in the 1930's; unlike Dorothy, Gordon descends into these worlds willingly. Like both Flory and Dorothy, Gordon's ultimate problem is whether to accept or reject society. But whereas Flory is finally "cast out" from his world and whereas Dorothy finally accepts hers as inevitable, Gordon's choice to accept society is conscious—and crucial to Orwell's purposes in this book. By the time of *1984*, the question of whether or not to "accept" society is, of course, moot. In that world, there are *no* choices.

This novel has also been judged, generally harshly, according to how the various critics respond to the character of Gordon; criticism becomes a popularity contest. For Hollis, Gordon is a "bitter fool," an "impossibly perverse, difficult, self-centered, unlovable man";[4] for Stephen Greenblatt, he is "obnoxious and detestable . . . narrow-minded, irritable, intolerant, ignorant, vain, arrogant."[5] For Wyndham Lewis, Gordon is merely "frightful."[6] Such judgments are understandable, perhaps, for Gordon is during much of the novel all that these terms imply and more; but such facile evaluations lead to misinterpretations of the book. Thus, it is said that "under the sheer weight of Gordon's ugliness" the theme of the novel is "smothered and forgotten."[7] One should instead say that Gordon's "ugliness," a result of the dominant force in the book—the power of money—is finally remedied at the end of the novel. Far from presenting Gordon's character as static and unchanging, Orwell renders the story of a man's education. Because of terms that Orwell himself employs, the book is best read as an "apprenticeship novel."

John Flory cannot accept or be accepted by society; Dorothy Hare accepts and is accepted, but, as Orwell makes clear, without much understanding. Gordon accepts a society he spends most of the novel denying. He finally comes to learn what Flory would not learn and what Dorothy was incapable of learning—and what Orwell expresses plainly elsewhere:

> The essence of being human is that one does not seek perfection, that one *is* sometimes willing to commit sins for the sake of loyalty, that one does not push asceticism to the point where it makes friendly intercourse impossible, and that one is prepared in the end to be defeated and broken up for life, which is the inevitable price of fastening one's love upon other human individuals.[8]

There is no question that the novel expresses this predicament and offers what Orwell suggests to be the proper solution. In moral and social terms, one may question such a resolution, but the steps in Gordon's movement toward that resolution should be first traced.

The opening scene of the novel, which introduces Gordon at his chosen job—clerk in a cheap, combination bookstore-lending library—suggests the place of *Keep the Aspidistra*

Flying in Orwell's development. Orwell continues the technique of the animal simile to suggest states of human behavior. An effeminate young man who has come in to browse holds a book "delicately between his pink nonprehensile paws, as a squirrel holds a nut."[9] Two lower-class women come in, looking like a "draggled duck" and a "plump little sparrow" (p. 10). As in *A Clergyman's Daughter*, the similes are generally random and without an informing context, such as the jungle in *Burmese Days*, to give them more than incidental interest. It is not until *Animal Farm* that this tendency to see the world as populated by human animals and animal humans becomes a fully integrated part of the book's structure. But another motif, only suggested in *Burmese Days* and *A Clergyman's Daughter*, is significantly developed into the fabric of this novel: the deliberate corruption of language. It is true that Gordon's chosen exile to the marginal poverty of lower-class London is an overt reaction to "the money-god"; for Gordon, "Money, money, all is money!" (p. 9). But though poverty is that against which Gordon is rebelling, his hatred is larger. Gordon really hates modern life, and modern life is symbolized by that most eminent agency for the corruption of language, advertising. He looks out from his shabby bookstore at "ad-posters" across the street, in which "Corner Table enjoys his Bovex" with the "face of a self-satisfied rat," "a docile little porker" (p. 15).

> He gazed out at the graceless street. At this moment it seemed to him that in a street like this, in a town like this, every life that is lived must be meaningless and intolerable. The sense of disintegration, of decay, that is endemic in our time, was strong upon him. Somehow it was mixed up with the ad-posters opposite. He looked now with more seeing eyes at those grinning yard-wide faces. After all, there was more there than mere silliness, greed and vulgarity. Corner Table grins at you, seemingly optimistic, with a flash of false teeth. But what is behind the grin? Desolation, emptiness, prophecies of doom. For can you not see, if you know how to look, that behind that

slick self-satisfaction, that tittering fat-bellied triviality, there is nothing but a frightful emptiness, a secret despair? The great death-wish of the modern world. Suicide pacts. Heads stuck in gas-ovens in lonely maisonettes. French letters and Amen Pills. And the reverberations of future wars. Enemy aeroplanes flying over London; the deep threatening hum of the propellers, the shattering thunder of the bombs. It is all written in Corner Table's face. (pp. 16–17)

Gordon is typically hyperbolic and self-pitying, indulging in drama for its own sake. Nevertheless, the terms of imminent disaster, the metaphorical equation from Bovex to bombing planes, and the image of the "thunder of bombs," which will dominate Orwell's next novel, Coming Up for Air, accumulate to make the advertising world the symbolic evil of the novel. At this point in his thinking, Orwell conceived the idea that corruption of language is an inevitable precursor of physical destruction. However, once that physical destruction arrives, in the fact of World War II, violence becomes comprehensible and strangely tolerable. The unbearable aspect of modern life will prove to be the corruption of language. But this looks far forward in Orwell's career, to the "Commandments" of Animal Farm and to Newspeak in 1984. In this novel, advertising is the evil that Gordon initially repudiates and ultimately accepts. To recall Orwell's words on Gandhi, advertising is the "inevitable price" that Gordon must pay.

But before he can pay that price, he must become aware of its meaning, and before he can understand this, he must be educated; as the novel's structure suggests, he must "grow up." There is little doubt that Orwell is heavily ironic toward Gordon, picturing him as a self-pitying adolescent of twenty-nine. In Mrs. Wisbeach's house, where he has a room, "tea-making was the major household offense, next to bringing a woman in" (p. 29); defiantly Gordon makes his own tea. But the description Orwell provides suggests a heavily ironic attitude toward this kind of self-proclaimed rebellion.

All clear! Gordon Comstock, poet ("of exceptional promise," *The Times Lit. Supp.* had said), hurriedly slipped
into the w.c., flung his tea-leaves down the waste-pipe and
pulled the plug. Then he hurried back to his room,
rebolted the door, and, with precautions against noise,
brewed himself a fresh pot of tea. (p. 30)

For the fact is that Gordon's self-imposed poverty and exile
provide no meaningful rebellion, positively alter nothing, and
only turn his private existence into one of loneliness and
despair. Gordon is "working" on a long poem, *London Pleasures*, a sardonic picture of the economic life of the time. But,
"it was quite certain, indeed, that it would never even be finished. And in the moment when he faced facts Gordon himself was aware of this" (p. 31). A distinction should be made
here. It is clear that Gordon voices many ideas that Orwell
held himself (e.g., the corrupting power of money, the banal
social life of London, the perversion of language implicit in
the advertising profession); at the same time this does not
make Gordon a thinly disguised or altered Orwell. Gordon
must learn, in effect, to unlearn some of these beliefs—at
least those beliefs which are unqualified and unrealistic.

The first two chapters of the novel establish Gordon's mis-
anthropic character and the nature of the situation into
which he has willed himself. At this point in the narrative,
Orwell interposes a chapter which recapitulates the history
of the Comstock family. The chapter seems at first superflu-
ous, as if Orwell were not sure whether Gordon's character
was credible without the justification of his environment and
heredity. But the thematic point of the chapter is that the
attitudes that young Gordon assumed and adopted are those
which he still holds at twenty-nine. At the third-rate private
school to which Gordon's mother sent him, literally killing
herself to raise the money, Gordon was abused by the other
boys because of his relative poverty, an experience Orwell
himself suffered and which he recounts in his bitter essay,
"Such, Such Were the Joys." The effect on Gordon is long-
lasting.

In a crude, boyish way, he had begun to get the hang of this money-business. At an earlier age than most people he grasped that all modern commerce is a swindle. Curiously enough, it was the advertisements in the Underground stations that first brought it home to him. He little knew, as the biographers say, that he himself would one day have a job in an advertising firm. But there was more to it than the mere fact that business is a swindle. What he realised, and more clearly as time went on, was that money-worship has been elevated into a religion. Perhaps it was the only real religion—the only really *felt* religion—that is left to us. Money is what God used to be. Good and evil have no meaning any longer except failure and success. (p. 43)

The symbol of the money-world is advertising, which Gordon comes to hate, and with it all the world of money; but Orwell stipulates that this attitude is "boyish." Nonetheless, Gordon systematically adopts it as his future way of life; in effect, the rejection of money becomes Gordon's religion.

Gordon thought it all out, in the naive selfish manner of a boy. There are two ways to live, he decided. You can be rich, or you can deliberately refuse to be rich. You can possess money, or you can despise money; the one fatal thing is to worship money and fail to get it. He took it for granted that he himself would never be able to make money. It hardly ever occurred to him that he might have talents which could be turned to account. That was what his schoolmasters had done for him; they had rubbed it into him that he was a seditious little nuisance and not likely to "succeed" in life. He accepted this. Very well, then, he would refuse the whole business of "succeeding"; he would make it his especial purpose *not to* "succeed." Better to reign in hell than serve in heaven; better to serve in hell than serve in heaven, for that matter. Already at sixteen, he knew which side he was on. He was *against* the money-god and all his swinish priesthood. He had declared war on money; but secretly, of course. (pp. 44–45)

The final phrase indicates Orwell's tone; at sixteen, "secret" wars against consummate frauds are understandable; private rebellions against public injustices are normal. At twenty-nine, Gordon's "war" in his loneliness and isolation is childish petulance, ineffectual and demeaning. Gordon's talents are wasted; he turns nothing to "account." He lives in an unproductive and futile way which is nothing if not "the frightful emptiness, a secret despair" which he himself describes as being the essence of the Bovex world. "The naive, selfish manner of a boy" enables Gordon to suggest two easy alternative ways of centering one's entire life. An adult, responsible world does not permit such a facile antinomy.

In thus willing himself to "despise" money, Gordon prescribes for himself life in a self-proclaimed "hell"; but it is, Milton notwithstanding, one in which Gordon neither reigns nor serves—he merely exists.[10] And the existence becomes progressively more grim. Finally even sex is seen by Gordon in terms of money. He is walking the streets, lamenting his loneliness, thinking of his girl, Rosemary Waterlow.

> He thought of Rosemary, of women in general, and of Rosemary again. All afternoon he had been thinking of her. It was with a kind of resentment that he thought of her small, strong body, which he had never yet seen naked. How damned unfair it is that we are filled to the brim with these tormenting desires and then forbidden to satisfy them! Why should one, merely because one has no money, be deprived of *that?* It seems so natural, so necessary, so much a part of the inalienable rights of a human being. (p. 103)

He meets Rosemary and (we are made to understand, "yet once more") tries to get her to promise to sleep with him. She will not; she "can't." Gordon, of course, translates this into his own obsessive frame of reference: "You won't sleep with me, simply and solely because I've got no money . . . if I had a decent income you'd go to bed with me tomorrow" (p. 114). That this is not really so, later developments prove: She declines him when his pockets are full of money, but gives herself to him willingly when he is again penniless. The obstacle is rather his own solipsism. He will not accept the conventional in her attitude, but is bound by it in his own. He is unwilling to go with Rosemary to a restaurant because he lacks money and when she offers to pay for her own meal, he refuses: "One can't do that sort of thing. It isn't done." Gordon, who rejects conventionality in others, who renounces middle-class social values and calls them corrupt, precisely bases his own actions on a quasi-Victorian system. And when Rosemary incredulously asks him if they are living in the reign of Queen Victoria, he replies that "Ideas don't change so quickly" (p. 118). Thus, Gordon lives in a world of contradicting, hypocritical values. Unwilling to believe that Rosemary could have other motives than money in refusing to sleep with him, he himself clings to moral notions much more prudish and outmoded than anything she demonstrates.

But Gordon finally worms a tacit promise from Rosemary that she will make love to him when they go on an outing to the country. At some expense (though, typically, more to others than to himself; he "borrows" five shillings from Julia, his hard-pressed, uncomplaining, and always-available sister) Gordon and Rosemary make the journey, leave the train, and walk into the countryside, happy amid the loveliness. The physical scene suggests Gordon's basic hopes (the beech trees are "curiously phallic"), but as well Gordon and Rosemary's initial incompatibility with this nature: "At first they felt shrunken and out of place, as Londoners do when they get outside London. Gordon felt as though he had been living underground for a long time past. He felt etiolated and unkempt."[11] They walk on for miles, Gordon noting the trees where the "knobs on the bark were like the nipples of breasts and that the sinuous upper boughs, with their smooth sooty skin, were like the writhing trunks of elephants" (p. 128). But a more elemental desire first overcomes them—hunger. They are forced to eat in an ostentatious, over-priced hotel, and, as usual, Gordon is so sensitive to his shabby appearance and limited money that he over-spends and over-tips—

almost as if "one must do that sort of thing." Their enthusi-
asm is naturally dampened; but after walking further on they
find themselves in an isolated copse, and the sun suddenly
breaks out. They begin to make love.

> For a long time he knelt and gazed at her body. Its
> beauty startled him. She looked much younger naked
> than with her clothes on. Her face, thrown back, with eyes
> shut, looked almost childish. He moved closer to her.
> Once again the coins clinked in his pocket. Only eight-
> pence left! Trouble coming presently. But he wouldn't
> think of it now. Get on with it, that's the great thing, get
> on with it and damn the future! He put an arm beneath
> her and laid his body to hers. (pp. 140–141)

There is indeed trouble coming, but it is not clear that the
cause of the trouble is the lack of money. At the crucial moment, it turns out that Gordon has no contraceptive, and so
their love is not consummated. As Rosemary seems a child
in her nakedness, so Gordon is a child in his reactions:
Though he admits that he "had not thought" of a contraceptive until that moment, he blames his inevitable target.

> There you are, you see! Money again! Even in the most
> secret action of your life you don't escape it; you've still
> got to spoil everything with filthy cold-blooded precau-
> tions for money's sake. Money, money, always money!
> Even in the bridal bed, the finger of the money-god
> intruding! (p. 142)

But Rosemary offers, as they continue their walk, to make
love without any contraceptive; she is willing to risk preg-
nancy. However, Gordon finds it "physically impossible"
when he has only eightpence left in his pocket.

Though we question whether he is prevented by poverty or
by his own personality, this scene does suggest the affective power of money. Rosemary calls Gordon "a baby," as
he reveals his economic impotence, and we are once again
reminded of the immaturity in his character. Rosemary's
love, her sacrifice (to her it is just that), her devotion—all

these mean nothing to Gordon. "She did not understand him; on the other hand, she forgave him everything" (p. 146). In Gordon's case, the terms are reversible: He understands as much as is necessary; he forgives nothing. He comes, in his penury, to deny all morality and decency—at the same time as he pretends a moral rebellion. Rosemary tries to tell him that having no money is not necessarily shameful. Gordon's reply indicates the moral emptiness to which he has sunk, the "underground" (a recurrent metaphor for Gordon's social atavism) world to which he has come; having no money is "the only thing in the world there is to be ashamed of" (p. 146). They return to London, and on the walk back to his home Gordon finds, under the stimulus of his bitter experiences of the day, the missing conclusion to his poem. It is the money-god

> Who binds with chains the poet's wit,
> The navvy's strength, the soldier's pride,
> And lays the sleek, estranging shield
> Between the lover and his bride.[12]

At this point in his "education," Gordon intellectually and poetically is unwilling or unable to accept responsibility. Living in a self-contained, self-centered world which is defined only by the success of rebellion against a convenient *bête noire*, Gordon is the same person at twenty-nine as he was at sixteen, when he "had declared war on money, but that did not prevent him from being damnably selfish" (p. 45).

The second major scene of Gordon's progress "underground" makes the shallowness of his beliefs clear. Immediately following his righteous re-renunciation of money, Gordon suddenly receives fifty dollars from an American periodical for the publication of one of his poems. The way he spends the money proves three facts: that Gordon is under the affective power of money; that his attitudes are sham; that he shares the same lower-middle-class values he so fanatically condemns. Though his conscience is troubled regarding his sister, to whom he owes much money and who is herself poverty-stricken, Gordon nevertheless takes Rosemary and his Socialist-Patrician friend Ravelston on a night on the town.[13] In an understandable, human way, given the length and depth of Gordon's poverty, he immediately squanders much of the fifty dollars on himself: "He did not go home for dinner. Why chew leathery beef in the aspidistral dining room when he had ten quid in his pocket—five quid, rather? (He kept forgetting that half the money was mortgaged to Julia)" (p. 154). But the great portion of the money is thrown away, figuratively and literally, in the course of a night of anchovies, roast pheasant, champagne—again understandably and humanly—but finally of squalid drunkenness and lechery. Gordon's behavior, ironically, makes him a more telling example of his theories than are any of the middle-class norms he so ridicules: He seems to prove that money does brutalize. But it is by no means clear that money is any more the culpable agent than his own puerile self.[14] Gordon, with the power of money now in his pocket, attempts to demonstrate to Rosemary his notion that the only reason she would not make love with him was because of his destitution. In revealing himself to be wrong, Gordon only reveals that *he* cannot use money.

> He thrust his hand right into the front of her dress. The movement was curiously brutal, as though she had been a stranger to him. She grasped that from the expression of his face. She was not Rosemary to him any longer, she was just a girl, a girl's body. That was the thing that upset her. She struggled and managed to free herself of him. He came after her again and clutched her arm. She smacked his face as hard as she could and dodged neatly out of his reach. (p.167)

After Rosemary, naturally hurt, leaves him Gordon drags unwilling Ravelston to an attempted assignation with two prostitutes. And the night ends as Gordon, ironically impotent even with his pockets full of money, passes out and is robbed. He wakes up the next morning in jail, dreadfully sick, to find that he has assaulted a policeman, that he is still dependent upon others—and to reveal that he is still a child. After a sergeant scathingly disdains the vomiting Gordon with the phrase "dirty little tyke," a constable takes care of him "almost like a nurse handling a child" (pp. 180–181). The consequence of the night is that Gordon loses his job and must live for a time at Ravelston's. Ravelston finally gets Gordon another job—again, he is helped by others—at a meaner and dingier bookstore: one of "those cheap and evil little libraries . . . deliberately aimed at the uneducated" which specialize in pseudo-pornography.[15] With lower wages, Gordon sinks down "in the safe soft womb of earth, where there is no getting of jobs or losing of jobs, no relatives or friends to plague you, no hope, fear, ambition, honour, duty —no *duns* of any kind."[16] In this squalor—"where he wished to be"—Gordon can conceive of duty and honor as "duns," can feel that in escaping from the overt manifestations of middle-class values he has at last found freedom from the money-based society that so obsesses him.

Gordon does not completely escape the bourgeois world, however. The aspidistra plant of the title is the recurring symbol which represents the middle class and its values. From the beginning of the novel, Gordon has had a "sort of secret feud with the aspidistra" (p. 28), a feud which parallels and symbolizes his running war with the money-god. But even now, in the "safe soft womb," the indestructible aspidistra cannot be avoided. No sooner has Gordon moved into Mrs. Meakin's filthy, bug-infested boarding house than she brings an aspidistra to his room, to make it "more 'omelike." Gordon feels but one consolation, which seems to affirm symbolically his belief that he has escaped the middle class: The aspidistra Mrs. Meakin brings him is "a poor weedy specimen—indeed, it was obviously dying" (p. 208). Gordon has, it appears, finally triumphed over the vestiges of middle-class morality. In his new sub-world he receives visits and offers of help from Ravelston, Rosemary, and from Julia. But he so disdains these overtures that he is gradually left alone in his torpor. He seems to have attained his wish, to go

"Down, down! Into the ghost kingdom, out of reach of hope, out of the reach of fear. Under ground, under ground!" As he reaches this state, the aspidistra dies and withers upright in its pot.

The apparent victory of Gordon's aspirations for the depths lasts less than a paragraph. For, though "surely *now* he was past redemption," Gordon simultaneously realizes that the "other world, the world of money and success, is always so strangely near. You don't escape it merely by taking refuge in dirt and misery" (p. 219). The "other world" does intrude—but it is a world of love rather than money. Rosemary arrives at his room, and, counterpointing her sympathetic lamentation over Gordon's newly turned grey hair—a suggestion of new maturity in the former "child"—they make love.

The next chapter begins three months later, in the spring, and we soon learn that the aspidistra has not died after all, but is blooming, and that Rosemary is pregnant. When Rosemary tells Gordon, his first reaction is that it is a "disaster"; "the thought of a baby, his baby growing in her womb had awoken in him no emotion except dismay" (p. 226). But when Rosemary offers to have an abortion, Gordon suddenly, and for the first time really, loses his egoism. "His eyes met hers. They had a strange moment of sympathy such as they had never had before. For a moment he did feel that in some mysterious way they were one flesh" (p. 226). Rosemary leaves, with no decision made. But the alternatives are clear: an abortion and things continue much the same; or they do not get married, and Rosemary returns to her home, in a small country town with an illegitimate child and the miserable life that implies; or they get married, and Gordon "turns respectable," and goes back to work for "New Albion," the advertising firm he had worked for briefly.

> If he went back to the New Albion, in a month's time he might be writing Bovex Ballads himself. To go back to *that!* Any "good" job was bad enough; but to be mixed up in *that!* Christ! Of course he oughtn't to go back. It was just a question of having the guts to stand firm. But

what about Rosemary? He thought of the kind of life she would live at home, in her parents' house, with a baby and no money; and of the news running through that monstrous family that Rosemary had married some awful rotter who couldn't even keep her. She would have the whole lot of them nagging at her together. Besides, there was the baby to think about. The money-god is so cunning. If he only baited his traps with yachts and racehorses, tarts and champagne, how easy it would be to dodge him. It is when he gets at you through your sense of decency that he finds you helpless. (p. 231)

The reference to Gordon's sense of decency—nonexistent up to now—suggests which solution he will accept. Before he can make the decision, he goes to a library, finds a book on the development of the foetus, and in effect "educates" himself further into the world of human beings, into the world of responsibility.

He pored for a long time over the two pictures. Their ugliness made them more credible and therefore more moving. His baby had seemed real to him from the moment when Rosemary spoke of abortion; but it had been a reality without visual shape—something that happened in the dark and was only important after it had happened. But here was the actual process taking place. Here was the poor ugly thing, no bigger than a gooseberry, that he had created by his heedless act. Its future, its continued existence perhaps, depended on him. Besides, it was a bit of himself—it was himself. Dare one dodge such a responsibility as that? (p. 234)

Turning to a newspaper, he is concurrently appalled by the advertisements, the world he must accept if he accepts his responsibility. "To be mixed up in *that*. To be in it and of it—part and parcel of it! God, God, God!" Nonetheless, "he knew already what he was going to do" (p. 235). He calls Rosemary, agrees to get a haircut; they are married. "Vicisti, O aspidistra!" (p. 240). But the victory of the aspidistra is not, in truth, unexpected or totally unwelcome. Once the decision is made, Gordon feels "nothing but relief"; his resolutions and principles, such as they were, now "seemed nothing but a frightful weight that he had cast off" (p. 237). He specifies that it was not merely the presence of the baby—that is, the demands of responsibility, the going out of his own self— which is the cause of new willingness to become part of the world. The baby may have been the immediate, "the precipitating cause"; but the true cause is a realization of the wrongness of the life he has been leading, a new, mature understanding of the demands of *this* world. Gordon's war with the money-god and the middle class had led him to a kind of living death; to Orwell this is a heinous sin, for it is wasteful and unnecessary.

> After all he did not lack vitality, and that moneyless existence to which he had condemned himself had thrust him ruthlessly out of the stream of life. He looked back over the last two frightful years. He had blasphemed against money, rebelled against money, tried to live like an anchorite outside the money-world; and it had brought him not only misery, but also a frightful emptiness, an inescapable sense of futility. To abjure money is to abjure life. Be not righteous over much; why shouldst thou die before thy time? (p. 237)

The religious metaphors are in terms of seclusion—and seclusion is wrong. They combine with social terms of maturation.

> He was thirty and there was grey in his hair, yet he had a queer feeling that he had only just grown up. It occurred to him that he was merely repeating the destiny of every human being. Everyone rebels against the money-code, and everyone sooner or later surrenders. He had kept up his rebellion a little longer than most, that was all. And he had made such a wretched failure of it! He wondered whether every anchorite in his dismal cell pines secretly to be back in the world of men. Perhaps there were a few who did not. Somebody or other had said that the modern world is only habitable by saints and scoundrels. He, Gordon, wasn't a saint. Better, then, to be an unpretend-

ing scoundrel along with the others. It was what he had
secretly pined for; now that he had acknowledged his
desire and surrendered to it, he was at peace. (p. 238)

The social language in which Gordon now thinks elevates the
once despised middle class to the status of the means by
which society is saved.

Our civilisation is founded on greed and fear, but in the
lives of common men the greed and fear are mysteriously
transmuted into something nobler. The lower-middle-class
people in there, behind their lace curtains, with their
children and their scraps of furniture and their aspidistras
—they lived by the money-code, sure enough, and yet they
contrived to keep their decency. The money-code as they
interpreted it was not merely cynical and hoggish. They had
their standards, their inviolable points of honour. They
"kept themselves respectable"—kept the aspidistra flying.
Besides they were *alive*. They were bound up in the
bundle of life. They begot children, which is what the
saints and the soul-savers never by any chance do. (p. 239)

The term "decency" is to be Orwell's highest praise.

Gordon's decision suggests yet another frame of reference.
Gordon may insist to Rosemary that they have an aspidistra
in their apartment, in a symbolic surrender to a world which
is now transformed from the evil money-god to the responsible middle class. But in terms first adduced in the climax of
A *Clergyman's Daughter*, Gordon's movement up from the
underground, even to the world of New Albion, is suggested
by Orwell to be something "customary, useful and acceptable." The crucial term for Gordon's case is, I think, "useful."
For Orwell states plainly that Gordon is a good copy-writer.
The product may be repulsive: in his job, Gordon takes part
in a campaign for the "Queen of Sheba Toilet Requisites
Co." in which the very successful slogan Gordon and his
superior invent is "P.P.," standing for "Pedic Perspiration."
But the point is that Gordon does this kind of work "very
well; he did it far better than he had ever done anything else

in his life" (p. 243). There is no doubt that Gordon was a bad poet; there is no doubt that he is a good advertising writer. At this stage in his thought, Orwell, who will always be very much the realist, seems to believe that no matter the cost man must accommodate his society. Those things that Gordon fought against are—abstractly and absolutely—bad. But *life* is not abstract and absolute, and life is what man must contend with. The coming baby brings life once again into the dreary monotony of Gordon's world: "Well, once again things were happening in the Comstock family" (p. 248).

Within a very short space of time, however, the acceptance of evil means for long-range positive ends, the willingness to live within a system of wrong values for the greater good of society, the realistic relativism that Orwell has stressed in his second and third novels, will be gone. The cost of accommodating society will have gone too high. The gentle, comic wrongs of New Albion will become transformed into a framework of absolute totalitarianism and oppression; the subjection of self to society will become an evil means rather than a positive goal. For Orwell's conception of the nature of modern society itself will become transformed. As Gordon is educated into social self-sacrifice, 1936, the year *Keep the Aspidistra Flying* is published, begins Orwell's own final education. In the winter of 1936, Orwell goes to Spain, takes part in the Spanish Civil War, and there comes to apprehend the political and moral beliefs which will dominate his work until his death, and which will raise him to the stature of a major writer. The apprenticeship has ended.

IV

HOMAGE TO
CATALONIA

> " 'The issues are very simple,' a young
> poet said to me at a party. 'This is a
> struggle between the forces of good in
> the world and the forces of evil.' "
> —Julian Symons, *The Thirties*

In the winter of 1936 Orwell, financed by an advance from Secker and Warburg, went to Spain to write his impressions of the Civil War. Once there, however, he immediately enlisted in the Republican army, an event he describes in his usual understatement: "I had come to Spain with some notion of writing newspaper articles, but I had joined the militia almost immediately, because at that time and in that atmosphere it seemed the only conceivable thing to do."[1] He remained in Spain until June, 1937, fought at the front, sustained a critical wound, and became involved in the internecine political struggles that endlessly plagued the Republican cause. These experiences are set down in his *Homage to Catalonia*, a book generally accepted as the best single account of the war in Spain, and a book which marks the turning point in Orwell's artistic development.[2]

Politics—or more exactly, the horrors of politics—is the theme of *Homage to Catalonia*, and Orwell's detailed examination of the specifics of the struggles among the Republican factions is an attempt to set the record straight, to record the political "truth" of the war as he lived it. His personal adventures, his insights into the individuals he encountered, the clinical way he examines his wounding—all these make this work readable and moving; but at the heart of the book exists Orwell's most extended examination of the problem with which he has been progressively coming to terms— the corruption of language. In this book, he attempts to show how fact becomes deliberately and disastrously distorted, and how this, rather than "the roar of bombs," is the central dilemma of a political century.

At first it seems Orwell is reluctant and piqued about the necessity of making the facts of the political struggles intelligible. Speaking of the factions, he says: "As for the kaleidoscope of political parties and trade unions, with their tiresome names—P.S.U.C., P.O.U.M., F.A.I., C.N.T., U.G.T., J.C.I., J.S.U., A.I.T.,—they merely exasperated me."[3] The catalogue of initials is obvious and effective humor; Orwell wants the war to be fought above factionalism and ostensibly petty distinctions: "I was puzzled and said: 'Aren't we all Socialists?' " Above all, his "attitude always was, 'Why can't we drop all this political nonsense and get on with the war?' " (p. 47). But a retrospective view finally brings Orwell to the realization that in fact the political war is the primary war, that this "political nonsense" has dire and dreadful implications for his society. Thus, the fifth chapter, putatively "digressive," is central to the book, marking a turning point in its structure. The first four chapters are primarily Orwell's rendition of the physical and emotional life he experiences in the tedium of trench-life. He details the facts of life on the front-lines: little action, cold, hunger, yet a kind of joy in the camaraderie of a socialist, meaningful war. However, the implications of an abortive Fascist attack described at the end of the fourth chapter are political. The Republican newspapers report a brief, desultory action as a "tremendous attack—with cavalry and tanks (up a perpendicular hillside!) which had been beaten off by the heroic English" (p. 44). This report provides Orwell with a transition by which he alters the focus of the book from the *facts* of the war to the lies about its *meaning*. He never abandons the book's chronological and biographical structure and the story is always that of his own experiences. Nevertheless, distortions by newspapers and official propaganda, both Republican and Fascist, and finally the almost insane reversal of ally and enemy become the predominant concerns.

These become central in Chapter Five, which Orwell apologetically says at the outset is at variance with the narrative of the war:

> At the beginning I had ignored the political side of the war, and it was only about this time that it began to force itself upon my attention. If you are not interested in the horrors of party politics, please skip; I am trying to keep the political parts of this narrative in separate chapters for precisely that purpose. But at the same time it would be quite impossible to write about the Spanish war from a purely military angle. It was above all things a political war. No event in it, at any rate during the first year, is intelligible unless one has some grasp of the inter-party struggle that was going on behind the Government lines. (p. 46)

The condemnation of the news media, usually the press, has been long present in Orwell's books. In *A Clerygman's Daughter* Dorothy Hare's encounter with Warburton, described in the headline as a "PASSION DRAMA IN COUNTRY RECTORY," is characterized as a "horrible, lying story" that "so unstrung her that it was impossible even for an instant to focus her mind upon anything else." Its "lickerish phrases" bring to Dorothy "such a pang that she wanted to cry out in physical pain."[4] Early in Orwell's development, he sees distortion of the truth as a source of pain and torture, even when limited to the effects upon a single individual; when active in a social world the implications are correspondingly broadened. The distortion of language is also an important theme in *Keep the Aspidistra Flying*, centering in Gordon Comstock's advertising "abilities," symbolically represented by

"P.P.: Pedic Perspiration." But it is not until Spain that Orwell comes to realize, or at least to articulate, the ramifications of these misrepresentations of fact and history. The need to establish somewhere "what really happened" becomes obsessive, as the personal imagination expands to a political scope. Language and politics have become inseparable.

The first political declaration Orwell makes is that what "had happened in Spain was, in fact, not merely a civil war, but the beginning of a revolution," that is, of course, a social revolution. This interpretation of the war, says Orwell, was a "fact" that had become the "special business" of the "anti-Fascist press outside Spain . . . to obscure" (p. 50). For example:

> In England, where the Press is more centralized and the public more easily deceived than elsewhere, only two versions of the Spanish war have had any publicity to speak of: the Right-wing version of Christian patriots versus Bolsheviks dripping with blood, and the Left-wing version of gentlemanly republicans quelling a military revolt. The central issue has been successfully covered up. (pp. 50–51)

The reasons Orwell gives for this deliberate simplification and falsification of the events in Spain are, one must say, equally simplistic: ". . . the main reason was this: that, except for the small revolutionary groups which exist in all countries, the whole world was determined upon preventing revolution in Spain." Orwell includes in this charge "in particular the Communist Party, with Soviet Russia behind it."[5] Though the charge is excessive, it seems explicable by Orwell's agonizing suspicion that the corruption of the secular Logos was imminent in the world. Although the remainder of the fifth chapter deals with the specifics of the internal factions of the Republican side (we learn to distinguish, as it were, among the alphabet groups), intermixed with this dissection are constant charges against the communication media, and no distinction is made between Left and Right:

> One of the dreariest effects of this war has been to teach me that the Left-wing press is every bit as spurious and dishonest as that of the Right. I do earnestly feel that on our side—the Government side—this war was different from ordinary, imperialistic wars; but from the nature of the war-propaganda you would never have guessed it. (p. 65)

One thought is constant: It is a just, noble war and cause—from the Republican point of view, of course; but of the perverting the history of the war both sides are equally guilty. Although now it may not even need saying, this theme points directly toward 1984, where the only difference is that the theme is fictionalized and made apocalyptic in implication. One example may illustrate the similarity of this theme in both books. Toward the end of *Homage to Catalonia*, Orwell is reporting the events of the Barcelona uprising, especially the harrassment of the P.O.U.M. and the Anarchists, and he describes the Communists' censorship of their newspapers:

> *La Batalla* was still appearing, but it was censored almost out of existence, and *Solidaridad* and the other Anarchist papers were also heavily censored. There was a new rule that censored portions of a newspaper must not be left blank but filled up with other matter; as a result it was often impossible to tell when something had been cut out. (p. 197)

In *1984* Winston Smith's job in the Ministry of Truth is concerned chiefly with the alteration of history; he clips newspapers and drops the offending, now nonexistent historical fact into a "memory tube." In *1984*, it is not merely "often impossible" to verify an historical occurrence, it is *absolutely* impossible; the society of *1984* allows no slip-ups. The slight difference between Barcelona, 1937, and Airstrip One, 1984, is only quantitative.

Likewise, the views in one of his later essays, "Looking Back on the Spanish War" (1943), are comparable to those in *Homage to Catalonia*. In this essay, Orwell again begins with the "physical memories, the sounds, the smells and the surfaces of things."[6] And as in *Homage to Catalonia*, he quickly moves to political considerations, defined initially through the misrepresentations, deliberate and otherwise, of the press.

> Early in life I have noticed that no event is ever correctly reported in a newspaper, but in Spain, for the first time, I saw newspaper reports which did not bear any relation to the facts, not even the relationship which is implied in an ordinary lie. I saw great battles reported where there had been no fighting, and complete silence where hundreds of men had been killed. I saw troops who had fought bravely denounced as cowards and traitors, and others who had never seen a shot fired hailed as the heroes of imaginary victories; and I saw newspapers in London retailing these lies and eager intellectuals building emotional superstructures over events that had never happened. I saw, in fact, history being written not in terms of what happened but of what ought to have happened according to various "party lines."[7]

This apprehension is identical to and perhaps more clearly articulated than the same idea running throughout *Homage to Catalonia*. Orwell develops the point in greater detail in this essay than anywhere else. The falsification of fact through both propaganda and reporting gives him "the feeling that the very concept of objective truth is fading out of the world."[8] From his extreme but justifiable distrust of the press in *Homage to Catalonia*, Orwell has moved to the very *impossibility* of the survival of truth, a tremendous leap that I contend is at the core of his entire intellectual development. He elaborates fully in the essay:

> I know it is the fashion to say that most of the recorded history is lies anyway. I am willing to believe that history is for the most part inaccurate and biased, but what is peculiar to our age is the abandonment of the idea that history *could* be truthfully written. In the past people deliberately lied, or they unconsciously coloured what they wrote, or they struggled after the truth, well knowing that they must make many mistakes; but in each case they

believed that "the facts" existed and were more or less discoverable. And in practice there was always a considerable body of fact which would have been agreed to by almost everyone. If you look up the history of the last war in, for instance, the *Encyclopedia Britannica*, you will find that a respectable amount of the material is drawn from German sources. A British and a German historian would disagree deeply on many things, even on fundamentals, but there would still be that body of, as it were, neutral fact on which neither would seriously challenge the other. It is just this common basis of agreement, with its implication that human beings are all one species of animal, that totalitarianism destroys. Nazi theory indeed specifically denies that such a thing as "the truth" exists. There is, for instance, no such thing as "Science." There is only "German Science," "Jewish Science," etc. The implied objective of this line of thought is a nightmare world in which the Leader, or some ruling clique, controls not only the future but *the past*. If the Leader says of such and such an event, "It never happened"—well, it never happened. If he says that two and two are five— well, two and two are five. This prospect frightens me much more than bombs—and after our experiences of the last few years that is not a frivolous statement.[9]

Remarkably, no one to my knowledge has specifically mentioned this passage as the core of the nightmare world of *1984*. The acceptance of the formula that $2 + 2 = 5$ is the endresult of the complete totalitarianism that pervades the book; when Winston Smith accepts this he has lost all. The significance of this passage is equally heavy for *Coming Up For Air* and *Animal Farm*, steps in the development toward *1984*. In *Coming Up For Air*, George Bowling, defeated in his attempt to recapture a pristine past, will return to his grimy present: "Why had I bothered about the future and the past, seeing that the future and the past don't matter."[10] In a world such as Oceania, where history is controlled, the future and the past indeed do not matter; George Bowling is a victim not so much of his inability to recapture the past as the impossibility of the past maintaining its integrity. *Animal Farm* also derives one of its major themes from this passage. As the original commandments by which the animals are to live are altered, those animals who try to retain some continuity with the past, who assert that the past indeed was different, are excluded from the present. Boxer's expulsion to the glue factory becomes "vaporization" in *1984*. However, the bases of the complete totalitarian world, not the particular forms of tyranny, are crucial. And the base of the worlds of *Animal Farm* and *1984* is discovered in the corruption of language in and about Spain.

This pre-eminent theme is not the only consistent motif that *Homage to Catalonia* reveals. From his first novel, most of Orwell's protagonists have been in one way or another "wounded." The pattern extends from Flory's birthmark to Dorothy Hare's amnesia; at one point, Gordon Comstock's self-enforced degradation leads to his becoming sick. After Orwell's return from Spain this basic metaphor remains, from George Bowling's obesity to Winston Smith's varicose ulcer. We obviously cannot attribute Orwell's own wound suffered in Spain to the existence in his imagination of the so-called symbolic wound, a constant in much of modern literature. But the prevalence of this idea in Orwell's mind prior to his own wounding may explain in part the amazing tone of the passage in *Homage to Catalonia* in which he describes both the wounding and his reaction to it. Although Orwell's tone is typically detached and impersonal, in this case the cold, clinical reaction to the actual experience is unusual. "I had been about ten days at the front when it happened. The whole experience of being hit by a bullet is very interesting and I think it is worth describing in detail" (pp. 184–185). Such occurrences may indeed be "very interesting," but the matter-of-fact analysis of such an event—"I had never heard of a man or an animal getting a bullet through the middle of the neck and surviving it" (p. 186)—is still disquieting to read, no matter how consistent is this quality of reticence in Orwell's prose style. He carefully remarks the feeling of the alcohol splashing on his neck; he notes the passage of time from the wounding to his realization that he may not die: "There must have been two minutes during which I assumed that I was killed. And that too was interesting—I mean it is interesting to know what your thoughts would be at such a time" (p. 186). One speculates that the wound perversely satisfied for Orwell some latent desire to experience the condition to which he had so consistently exposed his major characters: At last, he himself realizes the condition of physical discomfort, the actualized representation of the psychically alienated individual.[11]

But another approach to his wound is possible. Flory's birthmark in *Burmese Days* is a causal factor in his action; it seems to determine, at a crucial moment, his relationship with Elizabeth Lackersteen; it disqualifies him emotionally and socially from the community. On the other hand, Winston's wound in *1984*, similarly marking him as antagonistic to his society, is a saving grace: Winston is cured of his varicose ulcer in ratio to being cured of his antisocial behavior and indoctrinated into full acceptance of Big Brother's world; the healing of the wound becomes a metaphor by which Winston's loss of self-integrity is measured. As long as he suffers the sensuous awareness of pain, his outlaw self maintains its integrity, if for no other reason than that his consciousness of corrupt flesh reminds him his body belongs to a fate other than that determined by Big Brother. Though there is an obvious difference in the qualities of the two societies, Spain and Oceania, Orwell's wound seems to have become in his imagination a mark of his own humanity, and certainly it is not far-fetched to see this in his reaction to a wound honorably received in a just cause.

Thus, despite the grave political consequences for modern man which Orwell apprehends in this war, the tone of the book is largely determined by his personal involvement in the events of the war and by the manner in which he describes his experiences. Laurence Brander thinks the personal force of the narrative is the book's primary value.[12] Orwell's ex-

periences in Spain are indeed impressive though it seems to
me that the real value of this book is its effect on his development *after* Spain. Speaking of *Homage to Catalonia*, Sir Richard Rees says that "in spite of all the horrors, it is predominantly a gay book."[13] Such a term may seem ill-conceived, but
Rees is remarking here the undeniable fact that through
much of the book Orwell's tone is not the grim or exaggerated attitude that one has come to expect regarding a struggle
that even today continues to evoke passionate responses. The
accounts of the time spent at the front, in battle, and in the
interminable waiting are clinical and detached, and, to mod-
ify Rees's terms only slightly, there is ample evidence that
Orwell enjoyed certain elements. The book begins with the
rendition of an almost sentimental meeting, in the Lenin
Barracks in Barcelona, between Orwell and an Italian volun-
teer ("I hardly know why, but I have seldom seen anyone—
any man, I mean—to whom I have taken such an immediate
liking"), a meeting which Orwell says symbolizes the "special
atmosphere of that time" (p. 4). That "special atmosphere"
is a mixture of comic inefficiency and incoherence combined
with a fierce socialistic camaraderie. Orwell is sent to the
front, and there, as his company is unloading its gear, a rifle
shot is heard,

> . . . and one of the children of our company rushed back
> from the parapet with his face pouring blood. He had
> fired his rifle and had somehow managed to blow out the
> bolt; his scalp was torn to ribbons by the splinters of the
> burst cartridge-case. It was our first casualty, and, char-
> acteristically, self-inflicted. (p. 20)

This kind of event becomes symptomatic of the type of war
they are about to fight, and Orwell's response here becomes
typical of his attitude toward the war.[14] Descriptions of what
must have been extreme pain and terror are conveyed in a
way that radically qualifies the images of blood and destruction. The final phrase is mildly ironic, almost suggesting
humor. The terminology is technical, exact. Minor, seem-

ingly unimportant details focus the reader's attention on
the observer and his analysis rather than on the violence of
the incident. There is little qualitative difference between the
description of the accident to the boy and that of Orwell's
own near-fatal wounding. The presence of death and destruction is constant; at the same time, the rhetoric masks
the force of the scene by its scrutinizing tone. Nevertheless,
there are suggestions—implied by the imagery primarily—
that allude to a much more grim existence than Orwell will
overtly admit.

The seeming cavalier attitude toward the war, the veneer
of stoic indifference ("It was not bad fun in a way" in the
middle of describing a night attack [p. 96]) by which Rees
is so impressed—and I think deluded—is often in juxtaposition
with a description that devastatingly qualifies any "not bad
fun." Just prior to this comment, Orwell has said that he
remembers "feeling a deep horror at everything: the chaos,
the darkness, the frightful din, the slithering to and fro in
the mud, the struggles with the bursting sandbags . . ."
(p. 95). And immediately after this comment he describes
"the diabolical outcry of screams and groans" by a "poor
wretch," a Fascist incidentally, hit by a grenade Orwell threw
(pp. 96–97). This complex tonal mixture is constant within
the book and denies any simple tags such as "gay." Orwell
will movingly describe the incredibly dirty and spirit-shatter-
ing conditions of life in the mountain hovel which passes for
the front-line and immediately follow with a description of
the Nationalists and the Loyalists "fighting" by shouting
obscene insults at each other across the trenches.

Also creeping into the discussion of the war is a recurrent
pattern of animal imagery: The marching column straggles
along "with far less cohesion than a flock of sheep"; his
youthful comrades hurl obscene threats at the Fascists which
"sounded as pathetic as the cries of kittens" (p. 19); the hills
opposite his position in the lines "were grey and wrinkled like
the skins of elephants" (p. 25); the bullets "sang overhead
like birds" (p.31); the artillery guns sounded "with a deep,

muffled roar that was like the baying of distant chained-up monsters" (p. 85). This imagery, however it reinforces the helplessness of the individual soldiers amid the monstrosities of the war, and however it deepens the tone, is nothing extraordinary. The pattern culminates, however, in a passage which looks forward to a subsequent use of such imagery in an infinitely more serious way. Orwell returns to the front from the hospital, where he had gone for treatment of an infected hand, and takes part in an attack on Huesca, a Fascist stronghold.

> In the barn where we waited the floor was a thin layer of chaff over deep beds of bones, human bones and cows' bones mixed up, and the place was alive with rats. The filthy brutes came swarming out of the ground on every side. If there is one thing I hate more than another it is a rat running over me in the darkness. However, I had the satisfaction of catching one of them a good punch that sent him flying. (p. 83)

This incident which Orwell describes untypically in superlatives—it is the "one thing" he hates most—foreshadows the use of the rat torture in *1984* as the horror which causes Winston Smith to abandon his last vestige of individuality; for Winston, as for Orwell here, the fear of rats is the ultimate horror. Yet the difference between the two experiences is as strong as are the similarities; at this time, in this place, Orwell gives one of the rats a good kick; in the labyrinthine world of Room 101 there is no such defense, no such escape. The surface tone, clinical and objective, disguises somewhat the deep effect of the experience, a personal effect which is to be transformed into political torture only after the passage of years and the actualization of Orwell's political fears by the advent of World War II. In this barn, the incident seems isolated and managed, merely another indignity in a strenuous, a bad, but never an overwhelming time.

Other images relevant to Orwell's development occur in different contexts. A symbol important to much of his writing is described in the section detailing his night spent in the

ruins of a church, when he later returns to Barcelona, after
the political situation has worsened.

> I walked a long way and fetched up somewhere near the
> General Hospital. I wanted a place where I could lie down
> without some nosing policeman finding me and demand-
> ing my papers. I tried an air-raid shelter, but it was newly
> dug and dripping with damp. Then I came upon the ruins
> of a church that had been gutted and burnt in the revolu-
> tion. It was a mere shell, four roofless walls surrounding
> piles of rubble. In the half-darkness I poked about and
> found a kind of hollow where I could lie down. Lumps of
> broken masonry are not good to lie on, but fortunately
> it was a warm night and I managed to get several hours'
> sleep. (p. 213)

The scene of the ruined church, as Frederick J. Hoffman has
indicated, is almost an inevitable metaphor of the modern
age: secular and sacred combine, to effect the destruction of
the latter.[15] The hope of eternity suggested by the church
scene can become, as the treatment varies, either despairing
lamentation at the loss of such eternal promises, or a reaffirm-
ing belief that sees sacred values translated into secular contexts. For Orwell in Spain, the church is merely a refuge,
better than the air-raid shelter because it is more comfortable.
Now the church is finally ministering to the present; here, as
rubble, it serves a better purpose. The idea is not restricted
to this one passage in the book; Orwell makes several attacks
on the Catholic Church in Spain, both for supporting Franco
and for deluding the Spanish people.[16] This idea also appears
in 1984, where the first real refuge that Winston and Julia
find for their love-making is in the ruins of a church. Orwell
may have himself rejected the fact of the church; the metaphor, with its attendant suggestions of love and refuge from
secular terror, was not beneath his use.

Orwell also seems to discover in Spain a symbol which will
function in 1984 as another means of refuge from secular
politics—an artifact of the past through which a concept of
history is maintained. Orwell and his wife escape into France

when the anti-P.O.U.M. purge intensifies, having evaded an ineffectual search for political heretics at the border.

> My only souvenirs of Spain were a goatskin waterbottle and one of those tiny iron lamps in which the Aragon peasants burn olive oil—lamps almost exactly the shape of the terra-cotta lamps that the Romans used two thousand years ago—which I had picked up in some ruined hut, and which had somehow got stuck in my luggage. (p. 228)

This is near the conclusion of the book, and the symbolic value of the lamp provides almost the same force as Winston's prized paperweight in *1984*—concrete, ineradicable evidence of the past. The subject of much of the final portion of *Homage to Catalonia* is the recreation of the political terror that permeated Barcelona during the post-rebellion period. The means by which the terror is perpetuated—deliberate falsification—is one which Orwell has traced throughout. But given an artifact which concretely proves that the past did exist, both Winston and Orwell can cling to their versions of history, no matter what. In *1984*, of course, Winston's paperweight is smashed by the Thought Police. The ever present society of Oceania always impinges upon the privacy of the individual to assert *its* values, *its* version of the past. At this point, Orwell still affirms the existence of the private vision, the possibility of human sanctity. The basis of the end of human individuation is to be found in Orwell's experiences in Spain; but the articulation of this idea comes much later.

For human solitude, in varying degrees, dominates the last part of *Homage to Catalonia*. The narrative tells of the desperate attempt to free his friend George Kopp from prison where he had been incarcerated like so many other political unreliables. Orwell dashes about Barcelona in pursuit of a letter which will supposedly clear Kopp's political reputation; after much turmoil, he finally ferrets out the letter, but, almost predictably, it proves useless in getting Kopp freed. During these frantic days, Orwell is unable to stay with his wife in the hotel, for he is certain he is being hunted. He spends the nights alone, in various empty lots throughout Barcelona. But Orwell's own circumstances, which are surely more serious than they appear—again, the diffident tone masks the real dangers—only lead him to describe a far more threatening kind of solitude, Kopp's imprisonment.

> At the beginning we had two or three letters from him, smuggled out by released prisoners and posted in France. They all told the same story—imprisonment in filthy dark dens, bad and insufficient food, serious illness due to the conditions of imprisonment, and refusal of medical attention. I have had all this confirmed from several other sources, English and French. More recently he disappeared into one of the "secret prisons" with which it seems impossible to make any kind of communication. His case is the case of scores or hundreds of foreigners and no one knows how many thousands of Spaniards. (p. 227)

To insist that the horrors of Room 101 of the Ministry of Love grow out of only this situation is to overstate the case, for memories of the Nazi interrogations of World War II are undoubtedly operative in the background of 1984. But the combination of Orwell's own political isolation, the reiterated theme of the misrepresentation of the past, and the obvious effect that Kopp's arrest had on Orwell seem to me to be equally valid sources of 1984.

The closing pages of Homage to Catalonia describe Orwell's journey from Spain through Paris and back to southern England, back to what at first seems to be a return to a safe, unaffected past.

> Down here it was still the England I had known in my childhood: the railway-cuttings smothered in wild flowers, the deep meadows where the great shining horses browse and meditate, the slow-moving streams bordered by willows, the green bosoms of the elms, the larkspurs in the cottage gardens; and then the huge peaceful wilderness of outer London, the barges on the miry river, the familiar streets, the posters telling of cricket matches and Royal

weddings, and men in bowler hats, the pigeons in Trafalgar Square, the red buses, the blue policemen—all
sleeping the deep, deep sleep of England, from which I
sometimes fear that we shall never wake till we are jerked
out of it by the roar of bombs. (pp. 231–232)

The return is at first a return to history; the attempt is the
same as will be George Bowling's—to recapture the unspoiled
past. But the concluding statement, foreshadowing the impending war, denies the past, as "we" are "jerked" from the
sleep of historical continuity into a violent present. But as
"Looking Back on the Spanish War" reveals, when in 1943
Orwell has actually experienced this "roar of bombs," it
seems not so terrible. Understanding *Homage to Catalonia*,
we can see why the bombs are not to be terrible; their terror
has been superseded by a threat which exceeds immediate
force, a threat omnipresent in *Homage to Catalonia*—the
eradication of truth. After Orwell has known the horror of
trench warfare and has experienced the bombing of London,
he realizes that man's spirit can survive bullets, that cities
can be rebuilt, no matter how cities or spirits are altered in
the process. But the eradication of the very concept of a
thing, abstract or concrete, threatens external value in the
world and in the process inevitably denies personal integrity.

This, then, is the core of my reading of Orwell's works:
His Spanish experience (and its consequences) radically in-
fluenced his imagination. Certain basic ideas and certain basic
metaphors to express these ideas had been present in his work
from the outset. But he did not fully understand the consequences of these ideas and metaphors until he experienced
events and conditions which crystallized for him the significance of his beliefs, until what he saw in Spain made him
realize that his deepest fears were not only possible but were
actual. This realization changed his outlook on political
behavior in the twentieth century from parochial indignation
to apocalyptic despair. There is, finally, little difference between the fates of John Flory and Winston Smith: Total
isolation leading to suicide seems, if anything, preferable to

Winston's endless and mindless days. But there is a world of difference between the implications of the tyranny of the British Raj and that of Big Brother; it is the difference between personal ineffectuality and the enslavement of all civilization—and it was *Homage to Catalonia* that educated Orwell into this expanded universe.[17]

V

COMING UP FOR AIR

> "Father, this thick air is murderous. I
> would breathe water."
> —Sylvia Plath, "Full Fathom Five"

The concluding pastoral lines of *Homage to Catalonia*
where Orwell's imagination dwells on the halcyon English countryside of his childhood, the image of the
"roar of bombs" which enters to destroy the peace of this
"deep, deep sleep," and the implications of this landscape
combine to lead directly to Orwell's next book, *Coming Up
For Air*. This work brings to prominence a problem latent in
Orwell's career to this point, but one which will become critical from here on. With their respective strengths and failings,
Orwell's works of fiction prior to Spain have been for the
most part conventional novels. Though the early books are
criticized for various shortcomings, primarily the intrusive-
ness of the author's voice, there is no questioning their classification as novels. On the other hand, the three major works
which follow *Homage to Catalonia*—*Coming Up For Air*,
Animal Farm, and *1984*—have all been questioned on precisely the grounds of whether or not each is a "real" novel.
One approach to such criticism is to consider the effect of
Orwell's experiences in Spain upon his work. As he discovers
his fuller and more specific political insights in Spain, politics
are more consistently and successfully assimilated into the

fabric of his fiction. In turn, as the political concerns seem
to constrict to the theme of the corruption of language, so
does the scope of this theme widen—beyond, for example,
the relatively limited concerns of colonialism (as in *Burmese
Days*) or of organized religion (*A Clergyman's Daguhter*).
Now the political theme, more specific but greater in implication, becomes for the first time one with the fictive form. In
Orwell's final extension, the misuse of language is the theme
of the novel *1984* at the same time as it is Orwell's greatest
epistemological speculation.

This is a thematic justification; the question whether or not
Coming Up For Air is a novel can be approached through the
more technical matter of point of view. In *Coming Up For
Air*, for the first and only time in any of his six works which
are fictional (at this point I beg the question), Orwell employs the first-person point of view. The results bring widely
varying critical responses. To John Mander, the novel is a
failure essentially because of this point of view: The insights
and emotions that the narrator, George Bowling, expresses
are in reality only Orwell's, indistinguishable and even
derived from his essays.[1] Therefore the novel becomes for
Mander but a "documentary." Christopher Hollis uses the
same term when he charges that the book "has not really the
qualities of a novel one way or the other."[2] Even George
Woodcock, Orwell's most astute critic, feels that there is
an inconsistency between Bowling as a character and as a
"mouthpiece," "according to the rules of the game of novel
writing."[3] However, some critics see the point of view as
the means by which Orwell avoids his earlier pitfalls. Frank
Wadsworth remarks that "the first-person narration creates
an intimacy between Bowling and the reader, whom Orwell
frequently addresses, so that the typical Orwellian talkiness
no longer seems intrusive but an integral part of the character
of George Bowling." Bowling represents "a fusion of observa-
tion and imagination which in Orwell's career as a novelist
is unique."[4] But even though Wadsworth finds this agreeable,
I cannot accept his assumption that Orwell and not Bowling

is the narrator. Another commentator's acceptance of the point of view and its speaker is only slightly less complete.

> The story is told in the first person and the storyteller is designed to assist the comic atmosphere. He is a fat man, very garrulous, a little apologetic and with that touch of the pathetic which is the quiddity of the humour of fat men; George Bowling, an insurance company inspector, the countryman who has nailed himself down in a London suburb. He realizes what has happened to him and he has come to the middle forties when some men make a last struggle to escape. The idiom and vocabulary of the insurance agent are well maintained and agreeable and if at times the dry voice of Orwell the preacher echoes, a word or a phrase is introduced which restores the convention, and George Bowling is heard again.[5]

Whatever the particular assessment, each critic of the novel inevitably focuses on the question: Is George Bowling not really George Orwell? The general assumption is that if the two are the same, the novel is flawed, that it becomes, as Mander holds, a "documentary." If, on the other hand, one can separate the creator and the creation, even with the occasional lapses Brander remarks, the novel succeeds. Richard Rees finds *Coming Up For Air* "outstanding among his books in several ways," because while Bowling is "very unlike Orwell himself," he is a "plausible mouthpiece" for Orwell's own opinions.[6]

The point in discussion here seems related to certain fundamental assumptions about the nature of fiction in particular and art in general. Surely one assumption underlying the criticism of *Coming Up For Air* is the supposed distinction between "telling" and "showing." Authorial intrusion has become anathema; for the authorial voice to impose itself upon the drama of the work to comment upon the action or, a more grievous sin, to interpret the meaning of the action, has come to be the indication of failure. This is obviously back of Mander's ascription of *Coming Up For Air* as "documentary." In the addenda to his chapter on Orwell, called

"A Note on Documentary," he makes the distinction specific: "In the novel the author is present in his creation only in veiled, indirect, immanent form; in 'documentary' the author is a transcendent god who may visit and visibly interfere with his own creation."[7] If we accept this distinction, the list of books which are apparently no longer novels includes innumerable eighteenth- and nineteenth-century works, ranging from *Middlemarch* to nearly all of Dickens and Thackeray, from *Tristam Shandy* at the beginning of the history of the novel to *Sons and Lovers* today. Mander's definition is misleading and impossible; however, it is commonplace and accepted. And though a reading of his critical dicta reveals that Henry James explicitly denies holding to any other "obligation" for the novel than that "it be interesting,"[8] there is in my mind little doubt that it is James's influence—partly misunderstood—that is at the base of such strictures as Mander makes.

It is only recently that criticism has seriously examined the Jamesian inheritance. Wayne Booth's fine *The Rhetoric of Fiction* has, I think, demolished all the misconceptions that have accumulated since the late nineteenth century in regard to novelistic "constants." Booth comments on our immediate concern, authorial "commentary."

> But what, really, is "commentary"? If we agree to eliminate all personal intrusions of the kind used by Fielding, do we then agree to expunge less obtrusive comment? Is Flaubert violating his own principles of impersonality when he allows himself to tell us that in such and such a place one finds the worst Neufchatel cheeses of the entire district, or that Emma was "incapable of understanding what she didn't experience, or of recognizing anything that wasn't expressed in conventional terms"?[9]

Beyond this, as Booth points out, even if overt intrusions are eliminated the presence of the author is everywhere in a work of fiction, and the list of offenses to be expunged must logically be expanded to include all shifts of point of view from character to character within a given work. Then all "inside views" must be banned, since these are not realistic, but the product of an outside force; finally, at the logical extreme, the novel must be purged of "every recognizable personal touch, every distinctive literary allusion or colorful metaphor, every pattern of myth or symbol," for "any disconcerning reader can recognize that they are imposed by the author."[10] Booth—and I—push the argument to its extreme and, to be fair, it is an argument which critics such as Mander meet on their own terms when they accept the author's presence in the novel if it is veiled, indirect. But the point is that books in which the author is obtrusive, such as *Tom Jones*, may be more meaningful pieces of art, and more undeniably creative works of fiction, than a rigorously controlled, absolutely impersonally narrated book such as, to extend the argument again, a detective story. The presence of the author's voice, in and of itself, does not seem reasonable grounds upon which to base evaluation. The way in which the author uses his voice is proper matter for criticism.

A second assumption underlying judgments of this book also bears on the point of view and is also, and more legitimately, derived from Henry James. The Jamesian emphasis on showing rather than telling, explicitly demonstrated by Percy Lubbock,[11] led James into the extended development of his narrators or observers. Clearly, James's use of the narrator as a kind of "central conscience" is an impressive and important addition to the art of fiction. The use of the narrator to render another character's story is so deftly manipulated in James's hands that the moral and psychological ramifications created are profound. The formal rendition by, say, a Frederick Winterbourne or Lambert Strether of another character's story has only comparatively recently come to be understood in all its moral complexities. We now can see that the story is at least as much, and almost surely more, the revelation of Winterbourne as it is of Daisy Miller; the narration by Strether of the actions of Chad Newsome becomes itself the most important consideration—the shifting values of the perceiving narrator dramatize the principal themes of the novel, not merely the actions of the ostensible central figure. The techniques that James developed are great and long-lasting. But they may have had deleterious effects. I suggest that, in effect, James—and other influences I shall shortly adduce—has made the writer and critic wish for "unreliable narrators."[12] That is, the critic, conditioned by what he recognizes as great art in James, comes to feel that there must be distance between the narrator and his creator, that the narrator must be unreliable so that he can be distinguished from the author's norms and hence analyzed in contrast with these norms.

There are wider cultural and literary implications at the base of this demand for distance in the work of art. In what seems to be ultimately a reaction to romanticism, the twentieth century has codified the law of impersonality into dogma. The putative narrator, or the more fashionable "persona," has come to be *sine qua non* of art. We somehow feel suspicious of the overt speaking voice outside the essay form. The horrors of temporal experience are unendurable for the naked, revealed "I," and so the artist retreats, as does Hart Crane to the paradoxically impersonal subjectivity of private myth; as does Hemingway to a code of restraint within finite experience which enables the self to hide behind a set of prescribed manners; or, as does Joyce to mythical parallels and finally to the denial of any revealed self in the view of the world as dream. Only a D. H. Lawrence will continually assert the "I," for only a Lawrence feels that the ego can transform experience and history. Perhaps the preoccupation with the distance between the author and his work is one reason modern literature is obsessed with the concept of alienation. Stephen Spender sees the implications of the separation of the artist from overt participation in his work:

> . . . when the poetic "I" ceases to participate in a living community, that is to say to be the mouthpiece of a consciousness which is common to people who are close to nature, to heaven and hell, to birth and death, then it

becomes alienated from the wholeness of experienced
life. . . .[13]

I submit that impersonally narrated art can very well reveal
"the wholeness of experienced life"—that is precisely what
Joyce manages to achieve in *Ulysses*. But in practice impersonalness does maintain an esthetic distance that suggests
indifference to or separation from this wholeness. In a context of broader cultural implications, Frederick Hoffman
finds that in modern literature the detachment resulting
from the refusal to make a commitment to experience is "not
invalidly a consequence of depersonalization."[14] In a world
where all nonexistential values are suspect and where the individual self exists marginally, subject to forces and controls
of incomparable horror and power, the individual's sole
means of maintaining his concept of self becomes a series of
desperate alternatives: In Orwell, as we shall see, the means
becomes the experience of pain. To such measures is the individual driven in this century.

The discussion of the point of view in *Coming Up For Air*
has apparently taken us far afield. But I think the implications in Orwell's choice of point of view in this book are relevant to a reading of this novel and crucial to understanding
the development of Orwell's ideas. In a very literal sense, the
first-person narrator was absolutely necessary for Orwell at
this point in his career. The particular narrative form of *Coming Up For Air* signals the effect of Spain upon Orwell's intellect: his experience in Spain had educated him into the implications of his political concerns; he was now aware of the full
meaning of totalitarianism, of the full ramifications of political language; earlier themes of anti-imperialism and anti-
clericalism were now realized to be merely side-effects of a
much more grievously diseased body politic.

Further, for Orwell belief meant commitment and experience. One does not merely comprehend political tyranny
and then dramatize it in literature; one fights it in Spain. But

the experience of the civil war alters the form of the pre-Spain method of transforming experience into art. The actual experience is now missing; Orwell, in effect, lives in his work the experience of his imagination. Thus it is necessary to submit George Bowling to unmediated experience, without the distance and to Orwell the subterfuge of impersonal and unreliable narrative. This desideratum marks Orwell's place outside a main current of modern literature. In both his life and his work there is an active desire for engagement, involvement. He does not retreat behind a mask; he does not allow his heroes to evade "the arduous necessities of being."[15] He consistently submits his fictional characters to projections of his personal experiences. To a psychologist, the interesting facet might be the seeming need for discomfort to which Orwell subjected both himself and his protagonists. To the reader, the significant aspect is how this attitude is expressed in the recurrent pattern of the search in which Orwell and his characters have been involved—to Burma, to Paris and London, to Wigan. The trip to Spain and the experiences there are the critical moments in Orwell's intellectual development. These experiences become transformed in the late fiction to varied realizations—ultimately to full conception in 1984. But immediately following Spain, the particular search is intended to recapture the past. And the logical fictional form it takes at this point is another of Orwell's several journeys—the real journey to Spain now translated into the fictional journey as quest. Coming Up For Air is, at least in one respect, the central index for Orwell: Bowling's journey to recapture the past is foredoomed, and both we and he know it; nevertheless, the effort is made, for the self must be committed to the trial of the real situation, the real experience.

As the choice of the first person narrative in Coming Up For Air suggests wider literary and cultural implications, so does it serve within the book to reinforce theme. The narrative technique substantiates the ideas of the novel. Brander remarks that Part Two of the novel is "Orwell's only experiment in time." Although this is not completely accurate,[16]

the manipulation of time here does work effectively in con-
cert with the major action of the novel, Bowling's journey
to Lower Binfield. The beginning and ending sections of the
book form a frame in which Bowling's spatial journey is dramatically presented. But the journey also exists in time; this
more significant journey, to the past, is presented in the middle, flashback chapters. Thus the present surrounds, impinges
upon, and alters the past, and this is perhaps the central
theme of the novel. Bowling's trip to the Lower Binfield of
his childhood is a movement in space and in time, and the
middle parts of the novel affirm this once existent past—but
only as memory. For the reality of the present consistently
intrudes, placing the past in an altered perspective.

Bowling remembers and imagines the past; but the term
"nowadays" insistently encroaches on the normatively immutable fact of history. Affected by the constant assault of the
present, the recreation of the past is also denied by the future.
At the outset of the novel, Bowling is walking slowly up the
streets of London, watching the people, "all of them with
that insane fixed expression on their faces that people have
in London streets, and there was the usual jam of traffic with
the great red buses nosing their way between the cars, and
the engines roaring and horns tooting."[17] The feeling this
rouses in Bowling is "prophetic," a feeling which keeps
coming over him "nowadays," and so he looks "forward a
few years."

> I can hear the air-raid sirens blowing and the loudspeakers
> bellowing that our glorious troops have taken a hundred
> thousand prisoners. I see a top-floor-back in Birmingham
> and a child of five howling and howling for a bit of bread.
> And suddenly the mother can't stand it any longer, and
> she yells at it, "Shut your trap, you little bastard!" and
> then she ups the child's frock and smacks its bottom hard,
> because there isn't any bread and isn't going to be any
> bread. I see it all. I see the posters and the food-queues,
> and the castor oil and the rubber truncheons and the ma-
> chine-guns squirting out of bedroom windows. (pp. 30–31)

Bowling asks himself if he really believes that this kind of world is going to come about, and his reply is uncertain. "Some days it's impossible to believe it. Some days I say to myself that it's just a scare got up by the newspapers. Some days I know in my bones there's no escaping" (p. 31). But there is escape yet possible: Bowling suddenly sees a newspaper headline: "KING ZOG'S WEDDING POSTPONED." A "queer thing" happens. The name "ZOG" strikes a chord of memory in Bowling and he is suddenly "back in the parish church at Lower Binfield, and it was thirty-eight years ago" (pp. 31–32). At this point in the novel, the past is apparently recapturable. Bowling is conscious of the present in his recollection, but memory is still affective: "It had left a kind of after-effect behind. Sometimes when you come out of a train of thought you feel as if you were coming up from deep water, but this time it was the other way about, it was as though it was back in 1900 that I'd been breathing real air" (p. 35). Bowling believes that the present can be shaped by the past; action can be continuous. A man can make a meaningful journey to that past—in memory (that is, in time), and in space. George will return to his childhood town; this will establish the fact of the past; this will deny the overwhelming nature of the present. The hope is insistent; there is a will to believe. However, the result of the journey is knowing the impossibility of regaining the past, the impossibility of avoiding a vitiating present: "Why had I bothered about the future and the past, seeing that the future and the past don't matter" (pp. 277–278). All that exists is the present; but the present is, by its very nature, the beginning of the future. It is but a short step from Bowling's realization that the past is irreclaimable to the raw denial of history in *1984*.

> . . . I'd come to Lower Binfield with a question in my mind. What's ahead of us? Is the game really up? Can we get back to the life we used to live, or is it gone for ever? Well, I'd had my answer. The old life's finished, and to go about looking for it is just a waste of time. There's no

way back to Lower Binfield, you can't put Jonah back into the whale. I *knew*, though I don't expect you to follow my train of thought. And it was a queer thing I'd done by coming here. All those years Lower Binfield had been tucked away somewhere or other in my mind, a sort of quiet corner that I could step back into when I felt like it, and finally I'd stepped back into it and found that it didn't exist. I'd chucked a pineapple into my dreams, and lest there should be any mistake the Royal Air Force had followed up with five hundred pounds of T.N.T. (pp. 266–267)

Just as George's journey to time past is to be violated by the fact of the present, so is his quest for the spatial past denied by the change in Lower Binfield from a small, pastoral village into a modern, gross, industrialized suburb. Only one vestige of his childhood world remains, the small woods George used to play in: Now it has become a "sacrosanct" copse, set aside for children only—called "The Pixy Glen."

For the first time since *Burmese Days*, Orwell shows a conscious management of symbol. There are two primary symbols in *Coming Up For Air*: fish, general and specific, and the bomb, general and specific. Fish and fishing represent the past, the former days in Lower Binfield in George's childhood, and more specifically that part of the childhood which was an escape from the hardness of life even at the turn of the century: The pressure of his father's diminishing business, the grossness of his stupid brother, even the reality of the World War, all will vanish in the context of fishing. Bowling does not evade the reality of life in 1909:

It isn't that life was softer then than now. Actually it was harsher. People on the whole worked harder, lived less comfortably and died more painfully. The farm hands worked frightful hours for fourteen shillings a week and ended up as worn-out cripples with a five-shilling old-age pension and an occasional half-crown from the parish. And what was called "respectable" poverty was even worse. When little Watson, a small draper at the other end of the High Street, "failed" after years of struggling, his personal assets were £2 9s. 6d., and he died almost immediately of what was called "gastric trouble," but the doctors let it out that it was starvation. (p. 124)

But there is nonetheless something better in the past, something that people had that is lacking "nowadays": "a feeling of security, even when they weren't secure. More exactly, it was a feeling of continuity" (p. 125). The continuity with the past is symbolized by the feeling about fishing that Bowling maintains down to the present. Literally, this persistent feeling is all that links Bowling with the past he covets. But the actuality of fishing is, as is everything else, denied by time.

> Here I'll make a confession, or rather two. The first is that when I look back through my life I can't honestly say that anything I've ever done has given me quite such a kick as fishing. Everything else has been a bit of a flop in comparison, even women. I don't set up to be one of those men that don't care about women. I've spent plenty of time chasing them, and I would even now if I had the chance. Still, if you gave me the choice of having any woman you care to name, but I mean any woman, or catching a ten-pound carp, the carp would win every time. And the other confession is that after I was sixteen I never fished again.
>
> Why? Because that's how things happen. Because in this life we lead—I don't mean human life in general, I mean life in this particular age and this particular country —we don't do the things we want to do. It isn't because we're always working. Even a farm hand or a Jew tailor isn't always working. It's because there's some devil in us that drives us to and fro on everlasting idiocies. There's time for everything except the things worth doing. Think of something you really care about. Then add hour to hour and calculate the fraction of your life that you've actually spent in doing it. And then calculate the time you've spent on things like shaving, riding to and fro on buses, waiting in railway junctions, swapping dirty stories and reading the newspapers.

After I was sixteen I didn't go fishing again. There never seemed to be time. (pp. 93–94)

Bowling decides to "take" time, however, from his insurance selling to return to Lower Binfield, under the stimulus of fishing.

Why not, after all? I wanted peace, and fishing is peace. And then the biggest idea of all came into my head and very nearly made me swing the car off the road.

I'd go and catch those big carp in the pool at Binfield House!

.   .   .   .

I thought of it in the dark place among the trees, waiting for me all those years. And the huge black fish still gliding round it. Jesus! If they were that size thirty years ago, what would they be like now? (pp. 200–201)

The attempt to relive the past is, of course, doomed to failure. For the fish symbol and the images which attend suggest a mythical Eden—a dream world which actually never was, a private, perfect world in which time is stayed: The fish—a conventional symbol of fertility—has been "waiting" for Bowling. The novel specifically demonstrates this is a delusion.

The contrasting symbol, the bomb, logically serves a conflicting set of references. It primarily represents the future as the image of impending bombing pervades Bowling's mind, a graphic representation of the imminent outbreak of the war he prophesies. Bowling is riding the train to work in London, a "bombing plane flying low overhead. For a minute or two it seemed to be keeping pace with the train" (p. 19).

The train was running along an embankment. A little below us you could see the roofs of the houses stretching on and on, the little red roofs where the bombs are going to drop, a bit lighted up at this moment because a ray of sunshine was catching them. Funny how we keep on thinking about bombs. Of course there's no question that it's coming soon. You can tell how close it is by the cheer-up stuff they're talking about in the newspapers. I

> was reading a piece in the News Chronicle the other day
> where it said that bombing planes can't do any damage
> nowadays. The anti-aircraft guns have got so good that the
> bomber has to stay at twenty thousand feet. The chap
> thinks, you notice, that if an aeroplane's high enough the
> bombs don't reach the ground. Or more likely what he
> really meant was that they'll miss Woolwich Arsenal and
> only hit places like Ellesmere Road. (p. 22)

The imminent future becomes the immediate present in the
course of the novel, however, as a British plane accidentally
drops a bomb on Lower Binfield, at the moment when Bowling is strolling in the marketplace.

> BOOM—BRRRRR!
> A noise like the Day of Judgment, and then a noise like
> a ton of coal falling on to a sheet of tin. That was falling
> bricks. I seemed to kind of melt into the pavement. "It's
> started," I thought. "I knew it! Old Hitler didn't wait.
> Just sent his bombers across without warning."
> And yet here's a peculiar thing. Even in the echo of
> that awful, deafening crash, which seemed to freeze me up
> from top to toe, I had time to think that there's something
> grand about the bursting of a big projectile. What does it
> sound like? It's hard to say, because what you hear is
> mixed up with what you're frightened of. Mainly it gives
> you a vision of bursting metal. You seem to see great
> sheets of iron bursting open. But the peculiar thing is the
> feeling it gives you of being suddenly shoved up against
> reality. It's like being woken up by somebody shying a
> bucket of water over you. You're suddenly dragged out
> of your dreams by a clang of bursting metal, and it's ter-
> rible, and it's real. (p. 262)

The future has become reality, has become the present; the
bomb has replaced and denied the possibility of the fish, of
the past.

That the past and future will inevitably meet in the present
is foreshadowed in an early scene in the novel, in which
Orwell merges the two opposing symbols into a third, ironic

symbol. George has gone into a "milk-bar," where the atmosphere is "modern": "Everything slick and shiny and stream-
lined; mirrors, enamel and chromium plate whichever direc-
tion you look in. . . . Everything comes out of a carton or
a tin, or it's hauled out of a refrigerator or squirted out of a
tap or squeezed out of a tube" (pp. 25–26). George orders
a frankfurter, and bites into it.

> The frankfurter had a rubber skin, of course, and my tem-
> porary teeth weren't much of a fit. I had to do a kind of
> sawing movement before I could get my teeth through
> the skin. And then suddenly—pop! The thing burst in
> my mouth like a rotten pear. A sort of horrible soft stuff
> was oozing all over my tongue. But the taste! For a
> moment I just couldn't believe it. Then I rolled my tongue
> round it again and had another try. It was *fish!* I got up
> and walked straight out without touching my coffee. God
> knows what that might have tasted of. (p. 27)

Compared implicitly in their mutual shape, the bomb and
the fish merge in the frankfurter, and the modern world's
denial of the past pervades. Bowling, perceptive and yet nor-
mally colloquial—a truly realized characterization—connects
the two images.

> It gave me the feeling that I'd bitten into the modern
> world and discovered what it was really made of. That's
> the way we're going nowadays. Everything slick and stream-
> lined, everything made out of something else. Celluloid,
> rubber, chromium-steel everywhere, arc-lamps blazing all
> night, glass roofs over your head, radios all playing the
> same tune, no vegetation left, everything cemented over,
> mock-turtles grazing under the neutral fruit-trees. But
> when you come down to brass tacks and get your teeth
> into something solid, a sausage for instance, that's what
> you get. Rotten fish in a rubber skin. Bombs of filth burst-
> ing inside your mouth.[18]

The conflicting symbols merge in another, more meaningful pattern. Their full implications are best understood
through the subsumptive pattern of a mythical quest for

regeneration. In passages which have gone unremarked, there is a consistent impulse by Bowling toward symbolic rebirth through ritual immersion, contrasted by a pattern of movement toward the air. As he proceeds hopefully, Quixote-like in his mechanical Rosinante, toward Lower Binfield, Bowling confuses the water and the air, the movement up and down.

> I shoved my foot down on the accelerator. The very thought of going back to Lower Binfield had done me good already. You know the feeling I had. Coming up for air! Like the big sea-turtles when they come paddling up to the surface, stick their noses out and fill their lungs with a great gulp before they sink down again among the seaweed and octopuses. We're all stifling at the bottom of a dustbin, but I'd found the way to the top. (p. 198)

But the first sight of Lower Binfield denies the way upward. In fact, Lower Binfield has vanished, "swallowed" by an "enormous river of brand-new houses," buried somewhere in the middle of a "sea of bricks" (p. 211). The quality of potentially regenerative water is prefigured; what should promise rebirth instead suggests entrapment, entanglement—in just the same way John Flory was trapped by the stagnant, filthy water in *Burmese Days*. Bowling idealizes his journey as a way to escape to clean air, as he concurrently suggests a movement to water for rebirth. But both elements are fouled. The water is filled with tin cans, seaweeds, octopuses. In the air over what used to be Lower Binfield immediately appear a *fleet* "of black bombing planes" (p. 212).

In the past, in memory, water was untainted, truly regenerative; it was of a time that does not "belong to the modern world" (p. 87). In the past, all things are different.

> The still summer evening, the faint splash of the weir, the rings on the water where the fish are rising, the midges eating you alive, the shoals of dace swarming round your hood and never biting. And the kind of passion with which you'd watch the black backs of the fish swarming round, hoping and praying (yes, literally praying) that one of

> them would change his mind and grab your bait before
> it got too dark. And then it was always "Let's have five
> minutes more," and then "Just five minutes more," until
> in the end you had to walk your bike into the town because
> Towler, the copper, was prowling round and you could be
> "had up" for riding without a light. (p. 84)

Here time is controllable, constant before a youth which will
live forever in a pristine past. The religious language emphasizes a temporal immortality, a faith in an unchanging present, a never coming future. The past is immutable: It has
existed; it can never be changed. Before the actual experiences of Lower Binfield, Bowling can think wishfully, can
erroneously suppose that the pristine past may be maintained.

> I'd been fishing. I'd seen the float dive under the water
> and felt the fish tugging at the line, and however many
> lies they told they couldn't take that away from me. (p. 76)

The remembrance of the fishing is inviolate, thinks George;
the fact of memory cannot be denied. The Thames may be
"poisoned with motor-oil and paper bags"; the woods may
have been turned into an Anglicized Disneyland; even
Lower Binfield may have become "smothered under red
brick"; but "maybe the pool was still there . . . it was quite
possible . . . the kind of place most people don't care to pene-
trate. Queerer things have happened" (p. 250). But this is
self-delusion, a pathetic attempt at self-conviction; a momentary belief that things were "just the same" is obliterated by
the sight of the pool, turned into the UPPER BINFIELD MODEL
YACHT CLUB (p. 252). A second pool had been turned into
a "rubbish-dump" (p. 256).

Bowling comes to realize that "they" in fact can take the
past away, simply in the process of change. In the movement
of time, the facts of history become lost. Conscious of the
former importance of his family in the town, George is
momentarily surprised to discover that his name is not recognized in the hotel, that his father's Corn and Seed store has
become "Wendy's Tea Shop," and that his attempt at con-

versation with the proprietor about this change is taken as a sign of overfamiliarity. The way up and out of the modern world, already foredoomed in the images of bombers and smoke filling the sky, leads to a locus qualitatively similar to the rubbish-filled pool.

> What's the good of trying to revisit the scenes of your boyhood? They don't exist. Coming up for air! But there isn't any air. The dustbin that we're in reaches up to the stratosphere. (p. 157)

From this air, to confirm Bowling's realization, almost immediately falls the "accidental" bomb.

As the air and all it should mean has become a "dustbin," so does the water become not merely trash-filled, the result of the present spoiling the past, but a precise denial of any symbolic force of regeneration. The inexorable imposition of the future is now portrayed in images of a downward movement, into what was regenerative water. The future passes through the present and violates the past.

> The bad times are coming, and the stream-lined men are coming too. What's coming afterwards I don't know, it hardly even interests me. I only know that if there's anythink you care a curse about, better say good-bye to it now, because everything you've ever known is going down, down, into the muck, with the machine-guns rattling all the time. (p. 269)

After this realization, no movement is possible. The now lethal dustbin of air falls on Bowling, the present is forced down into the "muck." George can only return home, to his wife and children, to the domestic and social status he suffered at the outset of the novel. At the end of the novel, George considers alternative ways to placate his indignant wife; he decides to take his very immediate "medicine," for all he wants is the "line of least resistance" (p. 278). The technique of the novel has become the theme: There is no escape from the pressures of the "present tense"; the present

circumscribes the thought of the past and alters it to conform
to the imminent present. Only the present exists.

The intensity of George Bowling's futile search to recapture the past has been much remarked by commentators on
Orwell, for it suggests a strangely conservative political quality in a man who has become so nearly apotheosized by the
Left. Judgment about this apparent contradiction ranges
from censure to justification: Frederick R. Karl thinks that the
theme of recapturing the past is "sentimental" and "roman-
tic," and indicates Orwell's "alienation from major twentieth-
century literature and also acts as indirect comment upon his
kind of socialism."[19] Isaac Rosenfeld says succinctly: "He was
a radical in politics and a conservative in feeling."[20] The matter is somewhat more complex. The solutions to the social
problems in his first three novels were expressed in a clearly
conservative fashion, even though Orwell felt only disdain
for imperialism, organized religion, or for a capitalism which
perpetuates poverty among a great number of its population.
But the implications of Spain elevate social problems to a less
parochial plane: Those quasi-apothegms which he could con-
fidently fall back upon in his nonfiction do not seem sufficient in the fictional world after the realizations of the civil
war. Orwell may be able to quote Dickens with approval in
1939 (" 'If men would behave decently the world would be
decent' is not such a platitude as it sounds."),[21] but his fiction
from 1939 on rigorously denies the efficacy of such moralistic
slogans in the face of a growing sense of the power of evil
men and the ineffectualness of decent ones.

Orwell's literal exploration of the "possibility" of the past
in *Coming Up For Air* is the last and logical quest for a nexus
in which to fashion the formal alternatives and hopes in an
increasingly desperate existence. The political norms considered have proven futile: Socialism is workable, but, unfortunately, socialists are fallible humans. Personal relationships
are inevitably destroyed by human solipsism or the imposition of social forms. And the traditional mode of religious
faith is not possible for Orwell: "The real problem is how to

restore the religious attitude while accepting death as final."[22] In *Coming Up For Air* the quest, therefore, is for the stability and continuity of moral values. Even though in a supposedly more religious era of the past no one ever gave Bowling "the impression of really believing in a future life," people at that time knew "their way of life would continue. Their good and evil would remain good and evil." In a world in which spiritual rebirth is not possible, the values of the society itself remain the means of eternity: "It's easy enough to die if the things you care about are going to survive" (p. 126). But, inevitably after Spain, Bowling is wrong, at least in the hope that this cultural continuity will survive. It cannot endure even in the world of Lower Binfield and England of 1939, where the political powers are relatively disinterested (at least distant) and where there is no active malevolence. In Oceania in 1984, the existent malevolence is specifically directed at the extirpation of memory and continuity.

Coming Up For Air marks a transition for Orwell in many respects: It is the first novel in which the problems his characters face seem to have no solutions; the novel suggests that the alternative George Bowling seeks is no longer attainable. *Coming Up For Air* also is the first of Orwell's books in which the solution to the protagonist's problems has been essentially inwardly sought; social forms no longer seem worth even exploration—if survival in the modern world is to be found, it will come within the self. In a slightly different but related context, Leo Marx looks at the effect upon the individual of the machine in the modern world. The machine's increasing domination of the visible world

> compels us to recognize that the aspirations once represented by the symbol of an ideal landscape have not, and probably cannot, be embodied in our traditional institutions. It means that an inspiriting vision of a humane community has been reduced to a token of individual survival.[23]

For Orwell, the machine in question is politics, the mutability of language and hence fact in the hands of men—who, exactly according to a morality more traditional than he would have liked to admit, Orwell believed were inevitably corrupt.

A final problem remains, one which recurs in any consideration of Orwell's books. This is the question of tone: How are we to read this book—in terms of the implicit ideas or of the explicit characters? That is, is there not in *Coming Up For Air* a tone of lightness, of gaiety that refutes the dire implications I have been suggesting are present in the book? Hopkinson says the book is written "with dash and some enjoyment."[24] For Richard J. Voorhees the book is "a study in nostalgia," like the autobiographical writings of Twain and Mencken's *Happy Days*.[25] To Richard Rees, the situation is the same as Winston Smith's "but transposed into the key of comedy. . . . In spite of the depressing message its spirit is hopeful and humorous."[26] I cannot see how the "message" of a book is separable from its "spirit" unless one chooses to disregard the meaning of the "message."

But Rees's opinion indirectly suggests the complexity of Orwell's art and also, as if in answer to Karl, how very much Orwell is at the core of twentieth-century literature. In one of his overlapping definitions, Northrop Frye suggests that "the theme of the comic is the integration of society, which usually takes the form of incorporating a central character into it."[27] Bowling is reintegrated into his society, back into the "weeks on end of ghastly nagging," the "mental squalor" of his home. And it is apparent that the atmosphere of the last pages is primarily light: The domestic quarrel modifies the sense of great loss Bowling has apprehended. But perhaps Orwell's most profound insight, about either politics or art, is that in the twentieth century much—indeed, all—depends upon the nature of the society. To be integrated into a society which inflicts pain, or is evil, or demands evil is scarcely comic, in any but a satanically ironic sense of that word. Perhaps George Bowling's reintegration into his society promises no more horrible fate for him than it suggests for the rest of England, subjects him to no more moral or physical indignity than middle-class habits and relative economic well-being. Nevertheless, much is clearly lost in his return to the society which is "chromium" and which features fish-filled frankfurters, which, above all, is eradicating the fact of the past. George Bowling's reintegration may be couched in terms and contexts which only implicitly suggest deep horror, but it is abundantly clear that this terror is coming. It arrives in *1984*, in precisely the assimilation of Winston Smith into that society.

VI

ANIMAL FARM

> Life itself is essential assimilation, injury, violation of the foreign and the weaker, suppression, hardness, the forcing of one's own forms upon something else, ingestion, and—at least in its mildest form—exploitation.
>
> —Nietzsche

England was at war by 1940, and the publication of fiction was curtailed. Orwell had gone to work for the Far Eastern Service of the B.B.C. in 1941, where he remained, working "hard" until early in 1945.[1] However, these facts do not fully explain the hiatus in Orwell's fiction from *Coming Up For Air* in 1939 to the publication of *Animal Farm* in 1945. During this period, Orwell was writing a great deal; many of his most famous, his most important, and his best essays appeared. "Inside the Whale" (1940), "The Art of Donald McGill" (1942), "Looking Back on the Spanish War" (1943), and "Arthur Koestler" (1944) all appeared in this period; Orwell's sociological and patriotic tract, *The Lion and the Unicorn: Socialism and the English Genius*, was published in 1941. There appears to be a movement from novelist to essayist, to that genre in which Orwell is considered by many to do his best work.[2] We do know, however, that during this period he was working diligently on *Animal Farm*; it was, said Orwell, "the only one of my books I really sweated over."[3] Yet the "sweating" itself could not have been protracted, for Christopher Hollis reports that it was "written between November 1943 and February 1944."[4] A four-month period does not seem an especially lengthy period for a book which has been called a "masterpiece."[5] Between 1933 and 1939 Orwell had published a book a year, and his relative inactivity following this period is not easily explained, even by the war.

In "Why I Write" (1947), Orwell remarked that "*Animal Farm* was the first book in which I tried, with full consciousness of what I was doing, to fuse political purpose and artistic purpose into one whole."[6] Orwell's political purposes, though varied, had been consistently present to that point in his career; however, their infusion into his novels had been the obstacle he had to overcome to achieve fully realized and coherent art. The polemicist and essayist, concerned with political problems, causes, and effects, found the form of art difficult. And the struggle for appropriate form had become more crucial following Spain, as *Coming Up For Air* witnesses. For Orwell, politics had been a *sine qua non*; the common constituents of imaginative writing—character, image, narrative—were for him obstructions rather than guideposts. He is thinking of *Burmese Days*, for example, when he says that it is "invariably where I lacked a *political* purpose that I wrote lifeless books and was betrayed into purple passages, sentences without meaning, decorative adjectives and humbug generally."[7] Yet we also know that Orwell's impulses were toward "artistic purpose." Furthermore, his intention in the last years of his life was purportedly "to make a complete break from his former polemical, propagandist, way of writing and to concentrate on the treatment of human relationships."[8] Despite Hopkinson's notion of a "complete break"—obviously, given *Animal Farm* and *1984*, Orwell never denied politics completely—some purposes of the essayist never left him. But Orwell had come to realize that the stance of the polemicist, never long hidden even in his self-termed "naturalistic" novels, must be abandoned. And no form suited the abandonment of this role better than the beast fable: Not only was the narrator, the potential polemicist, gone, but the demands of the appropriate conventions provided an impersonality and distance which created art, not journalism.

That the beast fable was a natural choice for Orwell is borne out by John Wain. *Animal Farm* is

> . . . so remarkably similar in its tone, and in the balanced fairness of its judgments, to the critical essays as to be, almost, seen as one of them. It is, after all, a fable, and a fable is closer to criticism than to fiction in the full imaginative sense.[9]

Yet this is surely not the whole truth. Imagination must be given a more important role than Wain is willing to ascribe to it; and the underlying requirements of this form seem to me to run exactly contrary to "balanced fairness," indeed one of the consistent aspects in Orwell's essays. The essential characteristic of the beast fable is irony: The form provides for the writer "the power to keep his reader conscious simultaneously of the human traits satirized and of the animals as animals."[10] It demands of the reader a constant awareness of the double vision: Animal allegory prescribes two levels of perception which interact to purvey the irony in comparisons and contrasts. Orwell's essays are ironic only when they verge on fiction, as in the near-tales "A Hanging" and "Shooting an Elephant." In the kind of essays Wain has in mind, Orwell is honest and straightforward; the tone is that of the open, forthright speaker.

The use of this form provided an approach to art that Orwell clearly needed, one that differed from the conventional socially oriented novels he had been writing where he had fallen into pitfalls he now was recognizing. The need Orwell felt to criticize and attack social evils could now be subsumed into an artistic mode which by its very nature provided contrast and hence criticism. Paradoxically, the loss of a putative narrator and the gain of impersonalness that Orwell found in this form allow for a more intense criticism of social injustice and inequity than he had managed in his novels. The beast fable is in many ways the ideal form in which to articulate attack. The presence of beasts provides a ready-made vehicle for the tenor of the hatred in this essentially metaphorical mode. The correlation of a man, or a class of men, as swine or sheep allows savage hatred on the sub-narrative level and concurrently provides the coolness of impersonalness in the facade of the narrative. As I. A. Richards says of the properly functioning metaphor, the vehicle should not be "a mere embellishment of a tenor which is otherwise unchanged but the vehicle and tenor in co-operation give a meaning of more varied powers than can be ascribed to either."[11]

Whatever Orwell gained artistically with *Animal Farm* was matched by the popular success the book enjoyed. It was the first of his books to achieve substantial commercial success, was a Book-of-the-Month Club selection in the United States, had a large sale, and was translated into many languages.[12] Perhaps for the first time in his life, Orwell was moderately well off. The economic prosperity the book brought him was paralleled by critical accolades, and to this day *Animal Farm* is of all his works the most consistently praised. A judgment such as that of Frederick Karl, who finds the book a failure because of the "predictability" of the satire, is rare.[13] The consensus of approval is represented by a spectrum of praise that ranges from Tom Hopkinson's pronouncements that not only is it "by far Orwell's finest book,"[14] but it is one of only two present-day books so good that before it "the critic abdicates,"[15] to Sir Richard Rees's only slightly less enthusiastic encomium that the book is a "little masterpiece" in form and style.[16]

Because *Animal Farm* is so different from anything else that Orwell wrote, it is difficult to assess it in relation to his other works. It deserves much praise simply for succeeding despite the problems that this form and Orwell's particular use of it contain. I am thinking of the dangers of allegory in general and of the specific political allegory that informs *Animal Farm*. The principal danger of allegory in fiction is artificiality: The secondary level may demand such precise equivalents that it comes to dominate the tale, with the result that the primary narrative loses its pretense of reality and spontaneity. I think it is clear that this does not happen in *Animal Farm*. The allegory of the Russian Revolution and subsequent events is probably only noticeable to the eye which has been made aware of it.

Briefly, the narrative sets up equivalents with the history of political action in Russia from roughly 1917 to the Second World War. Major and Snowball are Lenin and Trotsky; Napoleon is Stalin; and the warring farms and farmers around Manor Farm naturally come to stand for Germany (Frederick) and the Allies (Pilkington). Certain events in the story are said to represent events of history: The timber deal, in which Frederick later reneges on the animals, is of course the short-lived Russo-German alliance of 1939; the card game at the end of the book is supposed to represent the Teheran Conference following the war. The correlations are more elaborate than this, and while there are some inconsistencies in the precise political allegory[17] it is notable that one need pay little heed to this to understand the book in its full political significance. Instead of being just an allegory of twentieth-century Russian politics, *Animal Farm* is more meaningfully an anatomy of all political revolutions. As A. E. Dyson says, *Animal Farm* "is by no means about Russia alone. Orwell is concerned to show how revolutionary ideals of justice, equality and fraternity always shatter in the event."[18] I would submit that the implications of this little book are wider yet: It is not merely that revolutions are self-destructive—Orwell also is painting a grim picture of the human condition in the political twentieth century, a time which he has come to believe marks the end of the very concepts of human freedom.

Nevertheless, the book starts with a relatively light tone. Mr. Jones—the commonplace name serves to diminish the importance of the human being in the story, yet gives a universal, "Everyman" quality—remembers to lock the henhouses for the night, but he is "too drunk to remember to shut the popholes."[19] The picture of the drunken farmer, drinking his last glass of beer for the night and lurching up to bed while the animals come alive in the barn, reminds us of the cartoons (and Orwell's interest in the popular arts is surely at play here) and is primarily low keyed; at the same time, however, we note the irresponsibility of the farmer, neglecting—and endangering—those in his care. Later Jones will neglect to milk the cows, biologically a more serious omission; later yet, the pigs will also forget the milking, an ironic parallel that reveals the subsequent corruption of the revolution at the same time as it makes the pigs like humans —at that stage of the revolution a heinous sin. Nonetheless, the meeting of the animals while the humans sleep, though latently serious, forms a picture which is primarily whimsical. The description of the animals gathering for the meeting reveals the essential technique of the beast fable: Our concurrent awareness of both human and animal qualities and the several ironies which this perspective creates.

> The two cart-horses, Boxer and Clover, came in together, walking very slowly and setting down their vast hairy hoofs with great care lest there should be some small animal concealed in the straw. Clover was a stout motherly mare approaching middle life, who had never quite got her figure back after her fourth foal. Boxer was an enormous beast, nearly eighteen hands high, and as strong as any two ordinary horses put together. A white stripe down his nose gave him a somewhat stupid appearance, and in fact he was not of first-rate intelligence, but he was universally respected for his steadiness of character and tremendous powers of work. (p. 16)

The contrast between the strength of the horses and the fragility of the smaller, hidden animals places the scene unmistakably in the beast world; at the same time, the description of Clover's failure to get back her figure, a phrase Orwell surely chose for its commonplace, cliche quality, is representative of radical human nature. The menagerie, in fact, demonstrates a spectrum of human qualities and types, from the pigs, who take up the front seats in the audience, to Benjamin the donkey, the cynic of the farm, and to Mollie, the white mare, vain and foolish. These introductory descriptions are woven into the structure of the plot: For her vanity, Mollie will ultimately be excluded from the farm; in his cynicism, Benjamin will come to see but be incapable of changing the reality of the revolution; and the pigs will come to occupy not only the front but the total of the farm.

The awareness of simultaneous levels of animal and human existence is nicely maintained by Orwell in all the story's aspects. Major's speech, describing his dream in which man has disappeared from the earth and is replaced by animals, is at once a logical demonstration of wish fulfillment in the dream at a bestial level and a gospel of economic revolution easily understandable at the human level. ("Man is the only creature that consumes without producing" is, of course, an ironic variation of Marxian anticapitalism.) Orwell reinforces this irony by having Major's speech full of biological analogies: "The life of an animal is misery and slavery: that is the plain truth. But is this simply part of the order of nature? Is it because this land of ours is so poor that it cannot afford a decent life to those who dwell upon it?" We slide back and forth between reading this as Marxian dogma, excoriating capitalism and calling for a proletarian revolution, and reading it in terms of the mistreated animals—and we are reminded of the irresponsibility of Farmer Jones.

Moreover, there is the possibility of a fourth kind of irony: In his reading of *1984*, Irving Howe remarks that Emmanuel Goldstein's book, *The Theory and Practice of Oligarchical Collectivism*, imitates Trotsky's style in "his fondness for using scientific references in non-scientific contexts."[20] Although there is a slightly different usage here, the employment of biological language in a political context is obviously related. We begin to be aware of the complexity of this seemingly simple little book. It is not simple political allegory, but neither is it merely classical satire built on multiple or "receding planes."[21] The various levels interact thematically: Animals are like humans; humans are, pejoratively, only like animals; human politics are really no more profound than natural biology.

The book is also constructed on a circular basis. Major's speech builds to the rhetorical climax of "All animals are comrades," which apothegm is immediately punctuated by the dogs' pursuit of some rats that they see. A vote is taken and the rats become "comrades," followed by the animals banding together against their common enemy, man, under the aegis of the motto, "All animals are equal" (p. 12). The remainder of the book will be a series of dramatic repudiations of these mottoes, a return to the tyranny and irresponsibility of the beginning. The only change will be in the identity of the masters, and, ironically, even that will be only partially changed.

At the opening of the second chapter Major dies, the prophet who articulated the revolutionary ideals and in whose name they will be carried out—and perverted. Snowball and Napoleon, two pigs, assume the leadership of the rebellion, aided by their public-relations man, Squealer. And these three codify the ideals of Major into Animalism, "a complete system of thought" (p. 18). But Animalism, obviously analogous to communism, is significantly instituted without any plan. The rebellion occurs spontaneously: Once again Jones neglects to feed the animals, who break into the barn for food when "they could stand it no longer" (p. 21). Jones and his hired man come in and the animals, "with one accord, though nothing of the kind had been planned beforehand," attack the men and chase them off the farm. "And so almost before they knew what was happening, the Rebellion had been successfully carried through: Jones was expelled, and the Manor Farm was theirs" (p. 23). Orwell stresses the spontaneity of the Rebellion to make clear that the social revolution per se is not the object of his satire. He emphasizes that no matter how bad things become for the animals later —and they do become bad—the animals "were far better off than they had been in the days of Jones" (p. 97). Though this fact will itself have to be qualified, there is a justness in the statement. Not only does the revolution's spontaneity diminish the importance of Napoleon and Snowball's plotting—and thus provide a dramatic irony about their supposed accomplishments—but the motive, hunger, justifies the revolution more basically and irrefutably than the soundest of political theories. The revolution sprung, not from theory, but from real, natural need. No matter how corrupt the ideals of the revolution become, Orwell never questions the validity of the uprising. The target here is not social—and socialistic—revolution, contrary to the many who simply want to see the book as a satire of communism, but rather the target is the inability of humans to live within a community of ideals.

The inevitable corruption of the revolution is presaged immediately. The animals have driven out their former masters.

> For the first few minutes the animals could hardly believe in their good fortune. Their first act was to gallop in a body right round the boundaries of the farm, as though to make quite sure that no human being was hiding anywhere upon it; then they raced back to the farm buildings to wipe out the last traces of Jones's hated reign. The harness-room at the end of the stables was broken open; the bits, the nose-rings, the dog-chains, the cruel knives with which Mr. Jones had been used to castrate the pigs and lambs, were all flung down the well. The reins, the halters, the blinkers, the degrading nosebags, were thrown on to the rubbish fire which was burning in the yard. So were the whips. All the animals capered with joy when they saw the whips going up in flames. (pp. 23–24)

The reaction is understandable; but the description of the inevitable and immediate violence that seems to follow all revolutions foreshadows that this revolution will suffer the common fate of its genre: reactionary cruelty, the search for the scapegoat, the perversion of the ideals of the revolution, and the counter-revolution. Thus, the good intentions of the animals are immediately endangered when it is learned that the pigs "had taught themselves to read and write from an old spelling book which had belonged to Mr. Jones's children."[22] The pigs' reading ability is a valuable skill for the animals, one which is necessary to run a farm, even for animals. But it is also patently a human attribute, and one which already violates one of Major's cardinal tenets: "Remember also that in fighting against Man, we must not come to resemble him" (p. 12).

If seeds of destruction are immediately present, the positive aspects of the rebellion achieve their high peak with the codification of the "unalterable law by which all the animals on Animal Farm must live for ever after," the Seven Commandments.

1. Whatever goes upon two legs is an enemy.
2. Whatever goes upon four legs, or has wings, is a friend.
3. No animal shall wear clothes.
4. No animal shall sleep in a bed.
5. No animal shall drink alcohol.
6. No animal shall kill any other animal.
7. All animals are equal. (p. 28)

This "unalterable law" provides the major structural basis for the rest of the fable. From this point on the plot reveals a gradual alteration of these commandments, ending in the well-known contradiction that epitomizes the new nature of the farm at the end of the book. But here, Orwell's technique is of immediate irony: The animals are watching the commandments being painted on the barn when the cows begin to low, needing to be milked. They are milked, and the milk is placed in front of the animals, at which many "looked with considerable interest." But Napoleon, "placing himself in front of the buckets," will not even mix it with the hens' mash, as "Jones used sometimes to," and it disappears, eventually into Napoleon's own mash. Selfishness is the note on which the chapter concludes, following the spontaneous and successful take-over of the farm and the articulation of unselfish ideals by which all the animals are to live.

The next concern on Animal Farm is to get the hay in, and we see further spoiling of the revolution's ideals as the pigs

supervise rather than work. From the beginning, all animals
are *not* equal. But one must be careful. In light of what is to
happen, it is easy to see that the pigs' managerial role is further foreshadowing of the ultimate perversion of the seventh
commandment, but this does not mean that the revolution
is therefore wrong, or that Orwell thinks that all revolutions
are inevitably self-corrupting. Both farms and revolutions
need leaders, managers; and, for all their evil, the pigs are the
most capable animals on the farm. Orwell may be suggesting—and this would be far more profound—that capable
people are inevitably evil; or, conversely, that evil people are
inevitably the most capable.[23]

The capability of the pigs, and their management, is
reflected in the success of the farm: There is no wastage, no
stealing. It is the biggest harvest in the farm's history; in
addition, though the animals work hard, there is no leisure.
Each animal works "according to his capacity" (p. 32). The
Marxian slogan at the base of the success of the farm seems
to me to prove conclusively that Orwell does not question
socialistic ideology. He does question the failure of ideology
to accommodate human variety, implicit in the missing half
of the quotation. At this point, Orwell specifically avoids
mention of what goes *to* each animal: The irony of "need"
is already apparent in what the pigs have taken and will be
reinforced by the future miniscule gains of the other animals.

Orwell further stresses the human variability which under-
mines the best—or the worst—of systems in the character of
Mollie, the vain mare more interested in ribbons than in
harvests, and in the description of the cat, who disappears
when there is work to be done. It is important that these
animals are portrayed kindly and humorously: The cat, for
example, "always made such excellent excuses, and purred so
affectionately, that it was impossible not to believe in her
good intentions" (p. 33). We soon learn the real nature of
these "good intentions." The cat is spied one day talking to
some sparrows who were "just out of her reach. She was telling them that all animals were now comrades and that any

sparrow who chose could come and perch on her paw; but the sparrows kept their distance" (p. 35). We are reminded again of the natural, biological basis of the revolution—and remembering this we cannot blame the cat. If this attempt by the cat is at one level an ironic mirror of the pigs' later, horrifying "education" of the puppies into vicious trained killers, it is simultaneously natural—which the pigs' deed is not. Orwell reminds us of natural instinct and its inevitable conflict with political absolutism. It is to the point that Mollie soon leaves the farm. She is seen one day being stroked by a human on the outskirts of the farm; Clover finds sugar and several ribbons hidden under the straw in her stall. And so Mollie disappears, to be seen pulling a cart, her coat "newly clipped and she wore a scarlet ribbon around her forelock. She appeared to be enjoying herself, so the pigeons said" (p. 53). In political terms, she is, of course, a heretic, and her selfish behavior is inconsistent with selfless social ideals. But there is no intention on Orwell's part to criticize her. He rather suggests that too strict attention to the harsh, social demands of life obscures the love of beauty in the world. Any criticism seems rather to be directed at a political norm which makes the esthete the apostate.

For political and social demands do dominate life at Manor Farm; and the demands become more complex. Pilkington and Frederick spread stories about horrible conditions on the farm, stories which are contradicted by rumors among their animals about the wonderful paradise that exists on Animal Farm. Neither set of rumors is true, of course, and Orwell develops the consequences of such misrepresentation. The Farmers' animals begin to revolt in varying degrees—"bulls which had always been tractable suddenly turned savage, sheep broke down hedges and devoured the clover . . . ," while the humans, hearing in the song of Animal Farm "a prophecy of their future doom," invade the farm (pp. 44-45). It is not the social situations or conflicting ideologies that Orwell concerns himself with, but the misrepresentations, the falsification and distortion of fact, which he indicates leads

ineluctably to disaster and misery. Falsification is at the heart
of the main internal struggle on the farm, and the way fact
is distorted and misrepresented is graphically pictured in the
rivalry between Snowball and Napoleon over the construction
of the windmill.

Snowball (who is a brilliant orator, compared with Napoleon, who was "better at canvassing support for himself in
between times") conceives of a plan for a windmill, which
Napoleon graphically disdains (he urinates on the plans). At
the meeting in which the final vote for approval is to be
taken, nine enormous dogs, "as ferocious as wolves," suddenly
appear and chase Snowball off the farm; the dogs return and
sit by Napoleon, wagging their tails, "as the other dogs had
been used to do with Mr. Jones" (pp. 60–61). And it is just
a short time until Squealer appears to announce blandly that
Napoleon, "who had advocated it from the beginning," himself proposes the building of the windmill. More is suggested
here than the simple power struggle attendant on all revolutions, or the more specific overthrow of Trotsky, the party
theoretician and planner, by calculating Stalin. The symbol
of the windmill suggests much about Orwell's complex attitudes toward the political concepts within the story well beyond the primary irony of the pigs' manipulation of the hopes
of Animal Farm's animals. The windmill has Quixotic overtones: Orwell suggests that the way the animals focus all their
efforts on building it is a false and deluded if heroic struggle.
The windmill becomes the means by which Napoleon controls deviation; he uses it to direct the animals' attention
away from the growing shortages and inadequacies on the
farm, and the animals ignorantly concentrate all their efforts
on building the windmill—but its symbolic nature suggests
an empty concentration, a meaningless, unheroic effort, for
the idea is literally misguided.

At the same time the symbol works in other directions.
The windmill is analogous in the political allegory to the
New Economic Policy. As such, it functions in much the
same way as do other symbols of secular paradise in twentieth-

century writing. Dams and bridges replace churches as representations of man's hopes for eternity; the windmill becomes a symbol of "secular heaven," placed in the future, but now in a temporal sense. I am reminded of Arthur Koestler's description of the Dnieper Dam, the "holy of holies," "a supernatural sight."[24] This image and others accrue in Koestler's mind until he can quote a young Soviet official as "wonderfully" summing up the younger Soviet generation.

> We are believers. Not as you are. We do not believe either in God or in men. We manufacture gods and we transform men. We believe in Order. We will create a universe in our image, without weaknesses, a universe in which man, rid of the old rags of Christianity, will attain his cosmic grandeur, in the supreme culmination of the species.[25]

While there is little doubt that Orwell was himself an atheist, I have reservations that he shared such a rhapsodic concept as the apotheosis of man to biological, social, and moral autotelicism. Organized religion and religious metaphors have been often used for varying purposes by Orwell prior to this book. Religious attitudes are thematically central to *A Clergyman's Daughter*: Religious metaphors are used for essentially ironic purposes in *Burmese Days*. In *Animal Farm*, precise religious satire is confined to Moses, the raven, who talks to the animals of "a mysterious country called Sugarcandy Mountain, to which all animals went when they died" (p. 20). Moses fled Manor Farm following the revolution, and when he returned later, he was "quite unchanged, still did no work, talked in the same strain as ever about Sugarcandy Mountain" (p. 128). The condemnation of religion is confined to its portrayal as an ineffectual force, with no real value, of no real harm. In *Animal Farm*, Orwell's secularism has no great need for the convenient metaphors that religion provides; the windmill is sufficient to suggest the hopeless transparency of the animals' goals.

The construction of the windmill, its subsequent destruction in a storm (during which the hens hear a gun go off in

the background; the allusion is probably to World War I),
and its rebuilding provide the linear movement of the plot in
the rest of the book. The thematic development is centered
on the progressive alteration of the Seven Commandments.
Two monstrous indignities are suffered by the animals, but
even these are thematically secondary. There is a bitter
winter on the farm and rations become scarce: "starvation
seemed to stare them in the face."[26] A scapegoat is needed,
and Snowball is conveniently used by Napoleon—who bla-
tantly tells the other animals that not only is Snowball
responsible for all the mysterious destruction that suddenly
begins to occur on the farm, but that his brave actions in
fighting the humans at the Battle of the Cowshed, which
all the animals witnessed, had never happened. This is, of
course, a direct prevision of the rewriting of history in 1984.
"Four days later," after being warned by Napoleon that
Snowball's secret agents are still among them, the animals
are ordered to assemble in the yard. Suddenly the dogs attack
four of the other pigs and Boxer; but Boxer easily fights
them off.

> Presently the tumult died down. The four pigs waited,
> trembling, with guilt written on every line of their coun-
> tenances. Napoleon now called upon them to confess
> their crimes. They were the same four pigs as had pro-
> tested when Napoleon abolished the Sunday Meetings.
> Without any further prompting they confessed that they
> had been secretly in touch with Snowball ever since his
> expulsion, that they had collaborated with him in destroy-
> ing the windmill, and that they had entered into an
> agreement with him to hand over Animal Farm to Mr.
> Frederick. They added that Snowball had privately ad-
> mitted to them that he had been Jones's secret agent for
> years past. When they had finished their confession, the
> dogs promptly tore their throats out, and in a terrible
> voice Napoleon demanded whether any other animal had
> anything to confess. (pp. 93–94)

In an obvious parallel to the purge trials of the 1930's, three hens come forward and admit to having heard Snowball speak to them "in a dream"; they are slaughtered. A goose confesses to pilfering six ears of corn, followed by a sheep who, "urged to do this" by Snowball, had urinated in the drinking pool, in turn followed by two more sheep who had murdered a ram. "And so the tale of confessions and executions went on, until there was a pile of corpses lying before Napoleon's feet and the air was heavy with the smell of blood, which had been unknown there since the expulsion of Jones" (p. 95).

Orwell has managed to dramatize, in two short, terror-laden pages, the very essence of this strange psycho-political phenomenon of our times: the ritualistic, honestly believed but obviously spurious confession., The ramifications of the motif in contemporary literature are many: One is reminded of a parallel such as Rubashov in *Darkness at Noon* and that, in a political age which denies individual selfhood, the only way of asserting one's self may be through pain or its extension, death. Ontologically and eschatologically, it may be preferable to die horribly and perhaps anonymously than to live as a cipher. However, I wish to consider the relative *insignificance* of the horrors that have passed, as physical terror becomes thematically subsidiary to the falsification of history and the denial of objective reality. Following this scene, the animals leave, led by Boxer and Clover. Boxer, unable to understand, thinks it "must be due to some fault in ourselves. The solution, as I see it, is to work harder" (p. 96). And so he trots up to the windmill to resume dragging loads of stone to it. The other animals huddle about Clover on the hillside.

> It was a clear spring evening. The grass and the bursting hedges were gilded by the level rays of the sun. Never had the farm—and with a kind of surprise they remembered that it was their own farm, every inch of it their own property—appeared to the animals so desirable a place. (pp. 96–97)

Clover, looking down on this scene, remembers the promise

and the hope of the revolution on the night she heard Major's speech, and her thoughts sum up the earlier images of the strong mare protecting the ducklings and recall the maxim at the base of the society, "Each working according to his capacity, the strong protecting the weak." Even here, she has "no thought of rebellion or disobedience," for the fundamental value of the revolution is reasserted: "Even as things were, they were far better off than they had been in the days of Jones" (p. 97). But the phrase "even as things were" implies too much, and so Clover, trying to somehow reestablish her continuity with that now quickly changing past, "feeling this to be in some way a substitute for the words she was unable to find," begins to sing the song, *Beasts of England*, which epitomized the egalitarian ideals Major expounded. The animals are singing the song when Squealer appears to announce that "by a special decree of Comrade Napoleon, *Beasts of England* had been abolished." Squealer tells the astonished animals that the reason is that "in *Beasts of England* we expressed our longing for a better society in days to come. But that society has now been established. Clearly this song had no longer any purpose" (p. 99).

The irony is of course the claim for a "better society," as the animals sit in the shadow of the heap of freshly slaughtered corpses. But the implications are more profound. Terror, bestiality, senseless death are all dreadful and shattering experiences; but they are at least comprehensible and do not radically alter the conceptualized values of the survivors. Far more terrifying is the overt alteration of consciousness which follows the slaughter, the blatant misrepresentation of the past, which goes unchallenged. The animals can only "sense" that the new song ("Animal Farm, Animal Farm/Never through me shalt thou come to harm") is different from *Beasts of England*. Squealer's pronouncement that the "better society" has now been established is uncontroverted. The commandments, which have begun to be altered recently, are now more rapidly and unquestioningly changed—and change pervades Animal Farm. A proposed timber deal vacillates between Pilkington and Frederick until the animals are forced to admit "a certain bewilderment, but Squealer was soon able to convince them that their memories had been at fault" (p. 107). Ironically, one of Major's prescriptions had been not to indulge in trade with the humans. Here the animals are not even sure whom the trade is with, much less can they remember past dogma.

The animals can no longer recognize reality, but they somehow manage to finish the windmill, concurrent with Napoleon's double-dealing with Pilkington and Frederick. We see the simultaneous strength and weakness, the goodness and corruption, that has evolved from the original rebellion. Despite all, the animals finish the windmill—they can accomplish a nearly impossible task—but at the same time, Napoleon, cheating and being cheated in his dealing, precipitates an attack upon the farm by Frederick and his followers (World War II, in the allegory). Though the animals win the battle, many are grievously injured and the windmill is destroyed. But Squealer declares that they have a "victory," "we have won back what we had before" (p. 116). And so the animals celebrate—each is given an apple, two ounces of corn for each bird, and three biscuits for each dog—while Napoleon gets drunk. The mere inequity, the surface irony is compounded by the inevitable falsification of fact. The next morning the animals discover that the fifth commandment did not read, as they had thought, "No animal shall drink alcohol," but instead "No animal shall drink alcohol to excess."[27]

It is not the threat of violence, even the radically inexplicable self-violence which the deracinated individual must, ironically, bring upon himself for his own secular salvation in a wholly political world, nor the war, nor the social injustice that man is suffering that is the cancer of our times, but the loss of "objective truth." Choices vanish in a society which has no bases for choice.

The most darkly pessimistic aspect of *Animal Farm* is that the animals are unable even to recognize their new oppression, much less combat it. The difference is that the pigs control language; Mr. Jones controlled only action—not thought. Orwell portrays at least three animals as being potentially able to stand up to the state (in an admittedly limited yet meaningful way), yet each is inadequate in a vital respect. Boxer has probably enough power and strength to overthrow Napoleon's regime. When Napoleon's vicious dogs attack him, Boxer simply "put out his great hoof, caught a dog in midair, and pinned him to the ground. The dog shrieked for mercy and the other two fled with their tails between their legs" (p. 93). But Boxer is stupid; he cannot comprehend the present, much less conceptualize the past. He ingenuously looks to Napoleon to see whether or not he should let the dog go; when the slaughter is over, he retreats to work, thinking the fault must lie within the animals. Thus, his fate is not as pathetic, as some critics read the scene in which he is taken away, kicking in the truck, as it is the inevitable fate of utter stupidity. The most complex thought that Boxer can express is "if Comrade Napoleon says it, it must be right," in the face of blatant, gross falsification. Boxer's basic goodness, social self-sacrifice, and impressive strength are simply inadequately used; the stupidity which wastes them suggests interesting qualifications about Orwell's reputed love of the common man, qualifications which become even stronger when considered in light of the descriptions of the proles in *1984*.

Clover is more intelligent and perceptive than is Boxer, but she has a corresponding lack of strength. Her "character" is primarily a function of her sex: Her instincts are maternal and pacifistic. She works hard, along with the other animals, but there is no picture of any special strength, as there is with Boxer. And even with a greater intelligence, her insights are partial. Things may indeed be better than they "had been in the days of Jones," but, in the context of the slaughter of the animals, "it was not for this that she and all the other animals had hoped and toiled" (p. 98). Both perceptions are right, but both are incomplete. In both cases, Clover senses that there is something further to be understood, but just as Boxer uncomprehendingly moves to toil, so does Clover wistfully retreat to song—only to have this articulation of the past's ideals suddenly changed, without her dissent. A paradigm appears: Boxer is marked by great strength and great stupidity; Clover has less physical power but has a corresponding increase in awareness; the equation is completed with Benjamin, who sees and knows most—perhaps all—but is physically ineffectual and socially irresponsible.

Benjamin, the donkey, "was the oldest animal on the farm, and the worst tempered. He seldom talked, but when he did, it was usually to make some cynical remark . . ." (pp. 5–6). As archetypal cynic, Benjamin remains aloof and distant, refusing to meddle in the farm's affairs, but seeing all. He expresses no opinion about the rebellion; he works on Animal Farm "in the same slow, obstinate way" that he did on Manor Farm; he only remarks enigmatically that "Donkeys live a long time" (p. 33). Beneath the surface cynicism, he is, almost predictably, blessed with a heart of gold: He is devoted to Boxer, and it is he who discovers the plot to deliver Boxer to the glue-maker. But Benjamin is essentially selfish, representing a view of human nature that is apolitical, and thus he can hardly be the voice of Orwell within the book, as some readers hold. To Benjamin, the social and political situation is irrelevant: Human nature suffers and prospers in the same degree, no matter who is the master. He believes "that things never had been, nor ever could be much better or much worse—hunger, hardship, and disappointment being, so he said, the unalterable law of life" (pp. 143–144). We know too much about Orwell's social beliefs from other contexts to assume that Benjamin speaks for Orwell here. Yet, it is only fair to note that Benjamin sees most, knows most, is obviously the most intelligent and perceptive of all the animals on the farm, including the pigs. To a certain extent, he represents intelligence without the effectuating and necessary strength; perhaps more profoundly, he demonstrates the Orwellian heinous sin of irresponsible intelligence. The posture of assuming that only the very worst is inevitable in life, that change for the better is a delusion, and that the only alternative is a retreat into a social self-pity is exactly the posture from which Orwell presumptively jerks Gordon Comstock in *Keep the Aspidistra Flying*.

With the means of opposition to Napoleon's totalitarian rule so portrayed, there is little suspense in the outcome of the situation the novel describes. Years pass. Jones dies in an inebriates' home; Boxer and Snowball are forgotten by nearly all, for a new generation of animals has grown up. The situation on the farm is unchanged for most of the animals. The farm is more prosperous now, but the fruits of prosperity never pass beyond Napoleon and his comrades. And the attempt to judge whether the present situation is better or worse than it had been under Jones is fruitless.

> Sometimes the older ones among them racked their dim memories and tried to determine whether in the early days of the Rebellion, when Jones's expulsion was still recent, things had been better or worse than now. They could not remember. There was nothing with which they could compare their present lives: they had nothing to go upon except Squealer's lists of figures, which invariably demonstrated that everything was getting better and better. (p. 143)

Again, the condition itself is not as depressing as the loss of the rational criteria which allow evaluation. The denial of memory enables control of the present, and hence of the future.

"And yet the animals never gave up hope" (p. 144). For they do retain one ineradicable achievement: equality. "If they went hungry, it was not from feeding tyrannical human beings; if they worked hard, at least they worked for themselves. No creature among them went on two legs. No creature called any other 'Master.' All animals were equal" (p. 145). The social and economic hopes of the revolution may have become lost in the actualities of history, but the primary political gain of the revolution remains valid for the animals. Orwell articulates this one, final achievement of the animals. But within a page Squealer and Napoleon appear, walking on their hind legs. Yet even this sight is not the final violation of hope. Clover and Benjamin walk around to the barn to read the seventh commandment:

ALL ANIMALS ARE EQUAL
BUT SOME ANIMALS ARE MORE EQUAL THAN OTHERS (p. 148)

After this, "it did not seem strange" that the pigs take the humans' newspapers, that the pigs dress like humans, invite neighboring humans in to feast and drink, that the name of the farm is changed back to Manor Farm, and that, in the final image of the book, the pigs become indistinguishable from the humans. The book has come full circle, and things are back as they were. If this is so, Benjamin's judgment becomes valid: Things do remain the same, never much worse, never much better; "hunger, hardship, and disappointment" are indeed the "unalterable law of life."

Power inevitably corrupts the best of intentions, apparently no matter who possesses the power: At the end, all the representatives of the various ideologies are indistinguishable —they are all pigs, all pigs are humans. Communism is no better and no worse than capitalism or fascism; the ideals of socialism were long ago lost in Clover's uncomprehending gaze over the farm. Religion is merely a toy for the corrupters, neither offensive nor helpful to master or slave. But perhaps more distressing yet is the realization that everyone, the good and the bad, the deserving and the wicked, are not only contributors to the tyranny, are not only powerless before it, but are unable to understand it. Boxer thinks that whatever Napoleon says is right; Clover can only vaguely feel, and cannot communicate, that things are not exactly right; Benjamin thinks that it is in the nature of the world that things go wrong. The potential hope of the book is finally expressed only in terms of ignorance (Boxer), wistful inarticulateness (Clover), or the tired, cynical belief that things never change

(Benjamin). The inhabitants of this world seem to deserve their fate.

One must finally ask, however, with all this despair and bleakness what are the actual bases for the tyranny of Animal Farm. Is the terrorism of the dogs the most crucial aspect? Is it this that rules the animals? Boxer's power is seen as superior to this violence and force. Is the basis of the tonal despair the pessimistic belief in the helplessness of the mass of the animals? Orwell elsewhere states again and again his faith in the common people.[28] It seems to me that the basis of this society's evil is the inability of its inhabitants to ascertain truth and that this is demonstrated through the theme of the corruption of language. So long as the animals cannot remember the past, because it is continually altered, they have no control over the present and hence over the future. A society which cannot control its language is, says Orwell, doomed to be oppressed in terms which deny it the very most elemental aspects of humanity: To live in a world which allows the revised form of the seventh commandment of Animal Farm is not merely to renounce the belief in the possibility of human equality, but in the blatant perversion of language, the very concept of objective reality is lost.

The mode by which the recognition of reality is denied is the corruption of language. When a society no longer maintains its language as a common basis by which value, idea, and fact are to be exchanged, those who control the means of communication have the most awful of powers—they literally can create the truth they choose. *Animal Farm*, then, seems to be in one respect only an extension of *Burmese Days*—the common problem is the failure of communication and its corollary, community. But if in *Burmese Days* their failure was contingent, in *Animal Farm* it is brought about by willful manipulation. The next logical step is seen in *1984*, where the consequences press to the premonition of apocalypse.

VII

1984

Power is wonderful; total power is totally wonderful.
—Madame Nhu

Following the end of the war, Orwell remained in London, now successful, working mainly as a journalist. He was ill, and was reportedly afraid of an impending atomic war.[1] His wife died in 1945, and Orwell was suddenly left with their adopted child. In an attempt to regain his health and to find some isolation in order to work, in 1947 he went to the island of Jura in the Hebrides, off the west coast of Scotland. He remained there for the most part—completing *1984* in 1949—until shortly before his death on January 23, 1950, in London. This biographical information is relevant only because Tom Hopkinson reports Orwell as himself saying of *1984*, "It wouldn't have been so gloomy . . . if I hadn't been so ill."[2] Indeed, *1984* is an unbearably gloomy work, describing and implying conditions and situations of horror and desperation that I think are unequaled in modern literature. I am not so convinced, however, that the book is significantly colored by Orwell's illness. It seems to me that *1984* is rather the inevitable culmination of Orwell's development; that, in effect, he had been progressing inexorably toward this book since his first essay was printed in 1931.

A problem more important than the impact of Orwell's

personal situation on the tone of the book is one raised by
Irving Howe, who questions whether or not *1984* is in fact
a novel.

> It is not, I suppose, really a novel, or at least it does not
> satisfy those expectations we have come to have with
> regard to the novel—expectations that are mainly the
> heritage of nineteenth century romanticism with its stress
> upon individual consciousness, psychological analysis and
> the study of intimate relations.[3]

The missing characteristics that Howe cites (to be fair, it
should be pointed out that he generally disputes this argument) are not necessarily essential criteria. This book does
have features which are, at the least, extraordinary to most
conventional definitions of the novel: The appendix of "The
Principles of Newspeak" and the long digression of Emmanuel Goldstein's (supposed) book, *The Theory and Practice
of Oligarchical Collectivism*. But these interpolations do not
necessarily prescribe the absence of, for example, "individual
consciousness." In one sense, the entire book merely portrays
successive alterations in Winston Smith's consciousness. Or,
to take another of the supposed lacunae in the book, even if
it is accepted that the study of "intimate relations" is absent
in significant degree, one of the major themes of the book—
the *impossibility* of any significant human relationship in the
world of Oceania—expressly justifies the relative absence of
relationships and the peculiar treatment of the relationship
between Julia and Winston. As Howe says, replying to the
supposed absence of any so-called three-dimensional characters in the book, "In *1984*, Orwell is trying to present the
kind of world in which individuality has become obsolete and
personality a crime."[4] I would argue further that *1984* is a
novel in the conventional sense of the term and as such is
as subject to the same forms of criticism as any other novel.

Believing that the political aspects of the novel are its only
substance has led critics to misrepresent Orwell's achievement. Richard J. Voorhees, for example, remarks that *1984*

p. 134

"is not really a novel at all. It is a combination of tale of
terror and political treatise." He substantiates this charge
with the oft-cited evidence of Newspeak and Goldstein's
book.[5] But as we shall see later Orwell uses Goldstein's
book to produce a highly effective dramatic moment within
the plot. It seems to me that these supposed interpolations
are assimilated into the fabric of 1984 in a manner superior
to, for example, that of the anti-imperialist pronouncements
in Burmese Days or the political-analysis chapters in the nonfictional Homage to Catalonia, which Orwell himself calls
journalistic.[6]

Nevertheless, 1984 is seldom recognized as a novel. Wyndham Lewis speaks for a substantial body of critics: "The
book as a whole is a first-rate political document."[7] One
response to this kind of statement is to consider the sources
and analogues of the book. 1984 is obviously in the tradition
of the utopian novel, and more exactly a late-nineteenth and
twentieth-century variation of that form, the "sour utopian"
novel. Within that broad spectrum, we can be certain of one
specific source, Eugene Zamiatin's We, first published in
1924. Writing in the London Tribune early in 1946, Orwell
praised We highly.[8] There are striking similarities between
We and 1984. As Isaac Deutscher points out, Orwell's own description of Zamiatin's society reads "like a synopsis of 1984."[9]

In the twenty-sixth century, in Zamiatin's vision of it, the
inhabitants of Utopia have so completely lost their individuality as to be known only by numbers. They live in
glass houses (this was written before television was in-
vented), which enables the political police, known as the
"Guardians," to supervise them more easily. They all
wear identical uniforms, and a human being is commonly
referred to either as "a number" or "a unif" (uniform).
They live on synthetic food, and their usual recreation is
to march in fours while the anthem of the Single State is
played through loudspeakers. At stated intervals they are
allowed for one hour (known as "the sex hour") to lower
the curtains round their glass apartments. There is, of

course, no marriage, though sex life does not appear to be completely promiscuous. For purposes of lovemaking everyone has a sort of ration book of pink tickets, and the partner with whom he spends one of his allotted sex hours signs the counterfoil. The Single State is ruled over by a personage known as The Benefactor, who is annually re-elected by the entire population, the vote being always unanimous. The guiding principle of the State is that happiness and freedom are incompatible. In the Garden of Eden man was happy, but in his folly he demanded freedom and was driven out into the wilderness. Now the Single State has restored his happiness by removing his freedom.[10]

Deutscher himself suggests other similarities between the two books, such as comparable means of torture, but another critic remarks a similarity which beyond any doubt links Zamiatin's book not only with *1984* but with the metaphor that has been at the center of Orwell's political and artistic thought since Spain. Frank W. Wadsworth notes:

When Zamiatin's uncertain hero ponders over "the source of right was—might! Right is a function of the might," we hear the voice of Winston's inquisitor, O'Brien telling his victim that "God is power"; when he struggles to understand the nature of reality in his mathematic world and writes, "There is but one truth, and there is but one path to it; and that truth is: four, and the path is: two times two," we recognize immediately the source of Winston's insistence that "Freedom is the freedom to say that two plus two makes four."[11]

Orwell had published "Looking Back on the Spanish War" in 1943; "Freedom and Happiness," in which he discusses *We*, was published in the first week of 1946. It is possible that he had read *We* prior to the writing of his Spanish Civil War essay, where the same equation occurs. But this is un-likely, and I know of no evidence to support it. Indeed, the tone of "Freedom and Happiness" indicates a recent reading: "Several years after hearing of its existence, I have at last got my hands on a copy of Zamiatin's We, which is one of the literary curiosities of this bookburning age."[12] When Orwell first heard of We, it is possible that this equation may have been mentioned; but in the absence of any more substantive proof, I submit that this common usage by two writers concerned with the same problem—the effects of absolute totalitarianism on individual consciousness—is best (perhaps only) understood as a coincidental realization of an image that graphically epitomizes the loss of human integrity under tyranny.[13] The destruction of all human reason is implicit in the statement that two plus two equal five. But the point at hand is generic, not thematic. If the theme implies great political insight it is also developed from Orwell's imagination. And the book, as we have seen, has other aspects which make its novelistic form clear. In summary, then, 1984 exists within an imaginative tradition dating back to Plato; it bears a clear, close relation with another book about whose fictional basis there is no question; and those conventional elements of the novel which I shall later trace in 1984 suggest that the book is most revealingly discussed as a work of art.[14]

The matter of Orwell's sources leads to another consideration within the book.[15] In 1946, Orwell published an article called "Second Thoughts on James Burnham," an essay-review of two of Burnham's books, The Managerial Revolution and The Machiavellians.[16] While Orwell's essay criticizes many of the predictions that Burnham makes, which Orwell saw time prove wrong, what is more significant is his commentary on many of Burnham's ideas—ideas which later become incorporated, in one form or another, in 1984. For example, as a basis of his The Managerial Revolution, Burnham asserts:

> Modern society has been organized through a certain set of major economic, social, and political institutions which we call capitalist, and has exhibited certain major social beliefs or ideologies. Within this social structure we find that a particular group or class of persons—the capitalists

or *bourgeoisie*—is the dominant or ruling class in the sense which has been defined. At the present time, these institutions and beliefs are undergoing a process of rapid transformation. The conclusion of this period of transformation, to be expected in the comparatively near future, will find society organized through a quite different set of major economic, social, and political institutions and exhibiting quite different major social beliefs or ideologies. Within the new social structure a different social group or class—the managers—will be the dominant or ruling class.[17]

These "managers" are later vaguely defined as "simply those who are, in fact, managing the instruments of production nowadays."[18] But more important than Burnham's thesis is what Orwell makes of it. At the outset of his essay he remarks Burnham's prediction that the new " 'managerial' societies will not consist of a patchwork of small, independent states, but of great super-states grouped around the main industrial centres in Europe, Asia, and America."[19] The division of the world in *1984* into the three conflicting states of Oceania, Eurasia, and Eastasia conforms closely to Burnham's divisions. Then Orwell cites Burnham as maintaining that "politics consists of the struggle for power, and nothing else."[20] When Orwell writes *1984*, he portrays the power mania as motiveless, a search for power as an end in itself. A third Burnham idea which Orwell remarks is one which occurred earlier, in *Animal Farm*; it is the notion that the most capable people, the "managers," are evil, or the converse, that evil people are the most capable.[21] He says that Burnham believes that "humanity is divided into two classes: the self-seeking, hypocritical minority, and the brainless mob whose destiny is always to be led or driven . . . according to the needs of the moment."[22] In *1984*, there are three divisions of humanity, but the Inner Party—clearly a small number of "managers"—controls the Outer Party, of which Winston Smith is a member, as ruthlessly as it controls the proles, who comprise eighty-five per cent of Oceania's population.

There is little doubt, then, that Burnham provided Orwell

with many conceptions which he altered to suit his own purposes. However, the final irony is the major criticism Orwell makes of Burnham when he says that Burnham becomes entranced with his own "apocalyptic visions."

> The slowness of historical change, the fact that any epoch always contains a great deal of the last epoch, is never sufficiently allowed for. Such a manner of thinking is bound to lead to mistaken prophecies, because, even when it gauges the direction of events rightly, it will miscalculate their tempo.[23]

It is perhaps because of this belief that the world of 1984 is created a priori. We do not see its development; we get little indication of how such a society came to be—and, importantly, the evidence presented in the book is a product of all-too-mutable history. Whatever the reasons, it is obvious that Orwell himself has dramatized an apocalyptic vision.

It is Orwell's vision of a future, not too distant but yet so radical in its departures from normative social experience,[24] that seems to me to be the reason critics are unwilling to treat 1984 in the way one should treat any political novel—as a novel. It is not the form of this novel that is inimical to convention and expectation, but its context. Orwell has pushed to the extreme the basic assumptions which govern man's condition: rationality, individuality, reality. The novel qua novel has not been pushed to any kind of reckoning, as, for example, one feels is the case with Finnegans Wake, though it does seem that this book was as far as Orwell himself could go. It develops to their ultimate state, all images, insights, and ideas which had been present in his mind since the writing of Burmese Days.

A brief consideration of three elements of Orwell's fiction will illustrate the relationship of 1984 to his earlier works. In looking at his novels we have noted the recurring motif of the "wounded protagonist": John Flory has his disfiguring naevus; Dorothy Hare suffers her attack of amnesia; Gordon Comstock, sick of the world, becomes physically ill; George

Bowling is hurt by an accidentally dropped bomb. (And, of course, Orwell himself is critically wounded in Spain, an event he describes at significant length in *Homage to Catalonia*.) One purpose of each of these disabilities is to separate the character from his society, to symbolically represent the alienation which, in varying degrees in each of the novels, later ends. Winston Smith, the "hero" of *1984*, also is "wounded": he suffers from a chronic cough and he has "a varicose ulcer above his right ankle" (p. 3).

Another image which has been consistently present in Orwell's earlier books is the church. In *Burmese Days*, the English Club is described in terms of a church, in an ironic reinforcement of the completely secularized world that exists in Kyauktada. Dorothy Hare is "a clergyman's daughter," and her father's church is one of the important symbols in that novel. In *Homage to Catalonia*, a ruined church becomes Orwell's refuge for a night; in *1984*, Winston and Julia make love in a bombed church. But what served primarily as symbol in the earlier works evolves to structure in *1984*. The novel is suffused with religious imagery, with secular—and profane—equivalents of religious ritual, culminating in Winston's death and rebirth into the heaven of belief in Big Brother. Unbelieving Winston Smith comes to know that "God is Power."

Two major themes will demonstrate Orwell's growth from inchoate perceptions to the full realization of his powers. John Flory renounces his maleness, in a pathetic offer, just to talk to Elizabeth Lackersteen, but communication fails; the misrepresenting newspaper in *A Clergyman's Daughter* is a prime cause of Dorothy Hare's amnesia and journey into the low-life of London and elsewhere; Gordon Comstock fights desperately to be a poet and to avoid going to work in a crass, commercial advertising firm, but finally succumbs. Misrepresentation leads to the realization of *Homage to Catalonia*, where Orwell is concerned not only with the failure of communication but with the corruption of language. And the corruption of language is the essential means of tyranny in *Animal Farm*. Simultaneously, the falsification of past and present fact has moved from a generalized concern with language in the early novels to clear statement about willful deception in *Homage to Catalonia*. In turn, this theme is portrayed graphically in *Animal Farm* in the alteration of the Seven Commandments and the instances of manipulating history. In *1984*, the two related strains meet and merge and finally are resolved, first into Winston's job at the Ministry of Truth rewriting history and finally into the "Principles of Newspeak." Plot has become theme has become dogma.

I have suggested a continuous and coherent development in Orwell's writing. But there is at the same time a clear difference between the fates of John Flory and of Winston Smith and the fates of Dorothy Hare and of Julia. What seems to remain constant is the isolated individual and the assimilating society; what changes following Spain is the nature and implications of the society and the means by which it controls its inhabitants. In *Burmese Days*, alienation leads to eventual destruction—no matter how loathsome may be the society that Flory covets; by the time of *1984*, alienation from that society has come to be the only means of (secular) salvation.

The opening paragraph of *1984* dramatizes that world, the society of Oceania.

> It was a bright cold day in April, and the clocks were striking thirteen. Winston Smith, his chin nuzzled into his breast in an effort to escape the vile wind, slipped quickly through the glass doors of Victory Mansions, though not quickly enough to prevent a swirl of gritty dust from entering along with him. (p. 3)

In choosing the most commonplace of English surnames and combining it with a Christian name obviously drawn from Winston Churchill, Orwell immediately suggests several things about his hero: He is Everyman and Anyman; his fate can be the fate of any citizen in this kind of society; at the same time, Winston Smith, like Winston Churchill, is

atypical in society—O'Brien later will say that his uniqueness
is the reason the Party takes so much pain to educate him
back to normality. Winston Smith is the potential hero of
the world of 1984, the man who can maintain his private
virtue against public demands; at the same time his surname
suggests that this is impossible, that he can ultimately only
share the fate of his fellowman.

As his name foreshadows the conflict Winston will undergo, so does the inescapable "gritty dust" represent the
grimy world of Oceania. Dust is the primary symbol of this
world and is used by Orwell as a principal element in the
structure of the novel. London, as Winston thinks about it,
is the "chief city of Airstrip One": ". . . the bombed sites
where the plaster dust swirled in the air and the willow herb
straggled over the heaps of rubble" (p. 5). Dust also char-
acterizes the inhabitants of London who have been fully
assimilated into the state. Mrs. Parsons, Winston's neighbor,
the mother of the two horrid children who are members of
the "Spies," a helpless, ignorant, grayish woman who stands
for the typical unthinking citizen of Airstrip One, gives Winston the "impression that there was dust in the creases of
her face" (p. 21). The image is exactly chosen by Orwell;
as he leaves her house, Winston "noticed with interest that
there actually was dust in the creases of her face" (p. 24).
Another early use of the symbol has added implications.
Amid the control devices, amid the thoughtscreens and enforced "Physical Jerks," which are torture for him, Winston
has committed an inconceivable crime: He possesses a diary;
he attempts to record history; he attempts to maintain a
physical link with the past.

> He put the diary away in the drawer. It was quite useless
> to think of hiding it, but he could at least make sure
> whether or not its existence had been discovered. A hair
> laid across the page-ends was too obvious. With the tip of
> his finger he picked up an identifiable grain of whitish dust
> and deposited it on the corner of the cover, where it was
> bound to be shaken off if the book was moved. (pp. 29–30)

In marking his diary with this piece of dust, Winston ironically places it under the control of the state. When the Thought Police come and examine the diary, while Winston still believes himself to be free, "even the speck of whitish dust on the cover of his diary they had carefully replaced" (p. 279). The dust represents both physical Oceania and the inevitability and totality of the state's power and control.

Thus, Winston's foray into the prole section of town, to try to find someone who can remember the past and thus empirically disprove any current "fact," ends in failure, as, in the logic of the book, it must. The old prole to whom Winston talks cannot help him, for he is feeble and his memory a collation of cliches; but this failure was inevitable, for they talk in a "dingy little pub whose windows appeared frosted over but in reality were merely coated with dust" (p. 86). Winston's attempt to subvert his world has twice been symbolically foredoomed to failure: Neither the diary nor the prole are free from control. The major attempt to defy the system, the love affair between Winston and Julia, is similarly haunted.

The relationship of Julia and Winston is the subject of Part Two of 1984. Their involvement is rapid: Julia, who has had many such liaisons, arranges their first rendezvous in the countryside (in a scene reminiscent of the journey of Rosemary and Gordon into the country in Keep the Aspidistra Flying). Winston is aware of the strangeness of the country surroundings, and we are aware, because of the dust symbol, that he is not free.

> The sweetness of the air and the greenness of the leaves daunted him. Already, on the walk from the station, the May sunshine had made him feel dirty and etiolated, a creature of indoors, with the sooty dust of London in the pores of his skin. (p. 120)

But their love-making, the "animal instinct, the simple undifferentiated desire," frees them dramatically. They are not captured; they arrange to meet again. And though in one of their meetings a rocket bomb drops near them and the explosion covers her lips with "some powdery stuff" and though "both of their faces were thickly coated with plaster" (p. 130), the use of the symbol seems to indicate no more than the background presence of the terror and war which pervade Oceania. However, as Winston seals his own fate in using dust to "protect" his diary, so does Julia symbolically doom their relationship. Efficient Julia, who handles all the details of how and when they are to meet, has them regularly switch meeting-places. She decides they may as well go back to the original spot in the woods. "And in her practical way she scraped together a small square of dust, and with a twig from a pigeon's nest began drawing a map on the floor" (p. 137). The next sentence places Winston in the "shabby little room" above Mr. Charrington's shop, and, as we soon find out, Mr. Charrington is a member of the Thought Police. It is not, of course, that the map of dust leads the Thought Police to Julia and Winston; the simple fact is that they have never been unwatched, have never had a chance. One of the problems facing Orwell in this book is how to provide dramatic suspense in a book in which the outcome is inevitable. One method he uses to maintain the suspense is just this symbolic pattern, providing an ironic counterpoint to the forlorn hopes that Winston and Julia articulate but never really believe, providing a symbolic clue which infuses the love affair with the quality of a pursuit.

Now fully committed to each other and simultaneously to eventual destruction, Winston and Julia share one more defiant delusion of freedom. O'Brien contacts Winston, Winston and Julia go to his home, and they are admitted to the—nonexistent, of course—Brotherhood, the supposed resistance organization. In this meeting, O'Brien clearly—and truthfully—reveals to Winston the ultimate fate of all heretics, and in the course of this conversation symbolically reveals himself to be a representative of the state's power.

> You will work for a while, you will be caught, you will confess, and then you will die. Those are the only results

that you will ever see. There is no possibility that any perceptible change will happen within our own lifetime. We are the dead. Our only true life is in the future. We shall take part in it as handfuls of dust and splinters of bone. (p. 177)

Winston and Julia's capture in the room above the antique shop takes place in another context of the dust symbol—one whose variation, however, suggests a new role for the state, that of punisher. A voice suddenly comes from behind the picture (of a church) on the wall. Thought Police burst into the room, and as the lovers are taken captive, one of the police picks up Winston's glass paperweight, "and smashed it to pieces on the hearthstone" (p. 224). The paperweight, with its coral centerpiece, has been a symbol of the past: a useless item, valuable only for its beauty, and therefore inimical to the society of Oceania; it proved to Winston that the past existed in a different form; it had specifically come to represent Winston and Julia's very existence. "The paperweight was the room he was in, and the coral was Julia's life and his own, fixed in a sort of eternity at the heart of the crystal" (p. 148). The "eternity" is ended, and in effect, Winston and Julia's life has become the smashed fragments of the glass, only a slight variation from "dust." The end of Part Two marks the end of the freedom of Winston and Julia, and with this loss the dust imagery largely vanishes—as it realistically should in the antiseptic and labyrinthine horrors of the Ministry of Love, the scene of most of Part Three. We encounter the dust image in a meaningful context once again, however. After Winston has been "cured" of his crimes and restored to the world of Oceania, living an empty, mindless life, he is given a new job: "Occasionally, perhaps twice a week, he went to a dusty, forgotten-looking office in the Ministry of Truth and did a little work, or what was called work" (pp. 296–297), on the latest dictionary of Newspeak. The cycle is complete and reassimilation is full: The dusty world of Oceania now has a properly functioning citizen.

A second symbol provides the contrasting element of the

book and finally merges with the dust to signal Winston's ultimate fate. Winston's varicose ulcer marks him as the last in the long line of Orwell's maimed protagonists stretching back to John Flory.[25] Flory's ugly birthmark primarily represents his unbreakable isolation from the society he covets; his acceptance into that society is only temporary, and he dies. Winston's varicose ulcer also represents his isolation from his society. It is temporarily healed in his love affair, as he moves out of his isolation, as Flory's naevus is forgotten in his heroism. But the wound in Winston's ankle becomes "active" again as he tries to maintain his individuality in the Ministry of Love, and is totally healed as Winston is "cured" back into society. Flory's naevus is never healed but persists in the history of memory after his death, asserting his personal value over the public values of his society. Winston lives—"well" and empty.

In the early part of *1984*, Winston's wound is associated with those activities that mark his deviation from the norms of Oceania: His primary crime is the possession of the diary and the attempt to record an unalterable picture of history.

> The actual writing would be easy. All he had to do was to transfer to paper the interminable restless monologue that had been running inside his head, literally for years. At this moment, however, even the monologue had dried up. Moreover, his varicose ulcer had begun itching unbearably. He dared not scratch it, because if he did so it always became inflamed. The seconds were ticking by. He was conscious of nothing except the blankness of the page in front of him, the itching of the skin above his ankle, the blaring of the music, and a slight booziness caused by the gin. (p. 9)

At this point Winston is only able to pour out "a stream of rubbish" describing his night at the movies in terms that repeat Oceania dogma. However, the very fact of writing anything down is apostasy, and this in itself is enough for the wound to inflame and mark Winston's criminal individuality. Later, Winston's perceptions are better focused, and as he copies a section of a children's history book into the diary he is aware of the inevitable failure of his attempt to record history. "Winston reached down and cautiously scratched his varicose ulcer. It had begun itching again. The thing you invariably came back to was the impossibility of knowing what life before the revolution had really been like" (p. 72). But, as he thinks about the impossibility of continuity with the past, punctuated by intermittently scratching his ankle, Winston remembers seeing three party functionaries in a cafe, which leads him in turn to remember that he had seen, in his job, a newspaper photograph of them in New York at the exact time which they had later confessed they were on Eurasian territory plotting against Oceania. Winston thus comes to understand that the state's willful mutability of the past is not merely the crime of rewriting history to accommodate the demands of the present, but is the very denial of human rationality.

> In the end the Party would announce that two and two make five, and you would have to believe it. It was inevitable that they should make that claim sooner or later: the logic of their position demanded it. Not merely the validity of experience, but the very existence of external reality was tacitly denied by their philosophy. (p. 80)

This insight leads Winston to a further heresy, which will be cured as the varicose ulcer is concomitantly cured.

> With the feeling that he was speaking to O'Brien, and also that he was setting forth an important axiom, he wrote:
> Freedom is the freedom to say that two plus two make Four. If that is granted, all else follows. (p. 81)

Winston's wound, the mark of his isolation and deviation from the world in which he lives, is temporarily assuaged as he comes to his relationship with Julia. Their first meeting is portrayed in the context of a wound. As Winston is at work one morning, he sees Julia coming toward him in the hall.

"As she came nearer he saw that her right arm was in a sling. . . ." She is drawing near, "when the girl stumbled and fell almost flat on her face. A sharp cry of pain was wrung out of her. She must have fallen right on the injured arm" (p. 107). Wounded Julia meets wounded Winston, and at this point she passes him a note which begins their relationship. Aware of the symbolic pattern, we can anticipate what will follow. As the two solitaries achieve a personal relationship, their wounds heal. For Julia, whose deviation from society is minimal—largely physical and therefore a minor threat to the state—the healing process begins almost as soon as the relationship is implicit. "The next day she reappeared. Her arm was out of the sling and she had a band of stocking plaster round her wrist" (p. 113). Winston's healing is not so rapid. Realistically it cannot be, of course; but more important, his complete healing back into the "health" of the state is the action of the remainder of the novel. Nevertheless, in his relationship with Julia—itself a heresy against the state—his wound improves.

> Four, five, six—seven times they met during the month of June. Winston had dropped his habit of drinking gin at all hours. He seemed to have lost the need for it. He had grown fatter, his varicose ulcer had subsided, leaving only a brown stain on the skin above his ankle, his fits of coughing in the early morning had stopped. (p. 151)

The pain in his ankle that Winston privately suffers and which diminishes is thus representative of his individuality. In an insight whose implications are terrible, Orwell asserts that pain is the sole cognitive mode by which a person can maintain his conception of self in a world in which selfhood is impossible. But there are kinds of pain; and Winston, becoming temporarily "well" with Julia, suffers a hint of another kind of pain, which is eventually to be healed by the state. With Julia he goes to O'Brien's home to be accepted into the Brotherhood. Then as Winston is about to leave, "O'Brien held out a hand. His powerful grip crushed the bones of Winston's palm" (p. 179). The external pain which the party wields is different from the pain that Winston's ankle gives him, and one is to overcome the other. The moment when the two kinds of pain meet occurs, as logically it should, when Winston and Julia are captured. When the Thought Police burst into the room above the antique shop, Julia is hit in the stomach, but Winston instead receives "a violent kick on the ankle which nearly flung him off his balance" (p. 224). This is the end of the second part of the novel, and the Party's punishment of Winston's individuality is to be followed immediately by their kind of pain, which is to lead him, ironically, back to their kind of health.

The torture Winston undergoes in the Ministry of Love avoids the former sign of his selfness: There is careful omission of the ankle among the parts of the body which the Party torturers abuse.

> Sometimes it was fists, sometimes it was truncheons, sometimes it was steel rods, sometimes it was boots. There were times when he rolled about the floor, as shameless as an animal, writhing his body this way and that in an endless, hopeless effort to dodge the kicks, and simply inviting more and yet more kicks, in his ribs, in his belly, on his elbows, on his shin, in his groin, in his testicles, on the bone at the base of his spine. (pp. 243–244)

Only once more does the varicose ulcer signify Winston's preserving his concept of self; this is after he tells O'Brien that he, a "superior" man, and more generally the "spirit of Man" will defeat O'Brien and what he represents. O'Brien ironically accepts Winston's challenge. "You are the last man," said O'Brien. "You are the guardian of the human spirit. You shall see yourself as you are. Take off your clothes" (p. 273). Winston looks into the mirror.

> A bowed, gray-colored, skeletonlike thing was coming toward him. Its actual appearance was frightening, and not merely the fact that he knew it to be himself. He moved closer to the glass. The creature's face seemed to

be protruded, because of its bent carriage. A forlorn, jail-bird's face with a nobby forehead running back into a bald scalp, a crooked nose and battered-looking cheek-bones above which the eyes were fierce and watchful. The cheeks were seamed, the mouth had a drawn-in look. Certainly it was his own face, but it seemed to him that it had changed more than he had changed inside. The emotions it registered would be different from the ones he felt. He had gone partially bald. For the first moment he had thought that he had gone gray as well, but it was only the scalp that was gray. Except for his hands and a circle of his face, his body was gray all over with ancient, ingrained dirt. Here and there under the dirt there were the red scars of wounds, and near the ankle the varicose ulcer was an inflamed mass with flakes of skin peeling off it. But the truly frightening thing was the emaciation of his body. The barrel of the ribs was as narrow as that of a skeleton; the legs had shrunk so that the knees were thicker than the thighs. (p. 274)

Then, O'Brien reaches over and with his fingers pulls a tooth out of Winston's mouth. After this realization of his complete physical domination by O'Brien and the Party, Winston has only his own inner conceptions to rely on. But these too are doomed. Just as the speck of dust on his diary revealed that book to be under the power of the state, so the Party now symbolically foredooms Winston to acceptance of their values by curing his wound. In language which is reminiscent of his fleeting moment of "health" and the loss of his isolation in his love of Julia, the state now becomes his healer and the eventual recipient of all his love.

He was much better. He was growing fatter and stronger every day, if it was proper to speak of days.

The white light and the humming sound were the same as ever, but the cell was a little more comfortable than the others he had been in. There were a pillow and a mattress on the plank bed, and a stool to sit on. They had given him a bath, and they allowed him to wash himself fairly frequently in a tin basin. They even gave him warm water to wash with. They had given him new underclothes and a clean suit of overalls. They had dressed his varicose ulcer with soothing ointment. They had pulled out the remnants of his teeth and given him a new set of dentures. (p. 277)

The final fragment of his old self that is left to Winston, that "inside" which has not changed as much as his appearance, is his belief that two and two equal four, the image which earlier in the novel had been used in the context of his varicose ulcer. Now his ankle is cured; the "curing" of his human reason comes quickly, and it is soon that Winston can write, and believe, that "Two and two make five. . . . He accepted everything. The past was alterable. The past never had been altered" (p. 280).

After the "surrender" of his mind, the only action left is the surrender of his "inner heart" (p. 283), which demands that Winston love not Julia but Big Brother. To this point, Winston has "not betrayed Julia" (p. 276). But Room 101 denies this last hope, the belief that "they can't get inside you" (p. 167), and so Winston's final surrender is complete and terrible. There seems to me no more profound rendering of the denial of human integrity and humane values in modern literature than Winston's final loss of self as O'Brien threatens him with torture by rats, for Winston "the worst thing in the world" (p. 286).

> "Do it to Julia! Do it to Julia! Not me! Julia! I don't care what you do to her. Tear her face off, strip her to the bones. Not me! Julia! Not me!" (p. 289)

The next scene finds Winston sitting at a "dusty table" in the Chestnut Tree Cafe. "Almost unconsciously he traced with his finger in the dust on the table: $2 + 2 = 5$" (p. 293). Winston is now "healthy," and the recurrence of the dust symbol indicates that he has attained the third stage in his "reintegration": "acceptance" (p. 264). Winston accepts—and is accepted.

The three stages of Winston's "reintegration" into the love of Big Brother are another aspect of 1984. Orwell's use of religious metaphors, chiefly for the purpose of irony, has been consistent in his work from *Burmese Days* to this point; the use of religion in *1984* has been noted,[26] but its pervasiveness in the novel has been generally overlooked.

The Two Minutes Hate, a daily ritual channeling the frustrations of the people of Oceania into mass hatred of the state's quotidian enemy, always ends in a picture of Big Brother, "full of power and mysterious calm."

> . . . the face of Big Brother seemed to persist for several seconds on the screen, as though the impact that it had made on everyone's eyeballs were too vivid to wear off immediately. The little sandy-haired woman had flung herself forward over the back of the chair in front of her. With a tremulous murmur that sounded like "My Savior!" she extended her arms toward the screen. Then she buried her face in her hands. It was apparent that she was uttering a prayer. (p. 17)

Orwell's purpose is satirical. He infuses religious metaphors into a completely secular context to suggest the corruption of the system, the perversion of eternal values by the ephemeral demands of politics. The transference of belief to Big Brother is profane—but inevitable in a world in which no sacred equivalents remain. A recurring image throughout the novel is St. Martin's church, one of the hazy, unrecallable images that Winston is always trying to locate in time past. But like any other aspect of the past it has "been put to other uses." It has become a "museum used for propaganda displays of various kinds—scale models of rocket bombs and Floating Fortresses, waxwork tableaux illustrating enemy atrocities, and the like."[27]

Orwell's own secular interests indicate that it is the *kind* of use to which religious metaphors and symbols are put that determines value, for the bombed church in which Winston and Julia make love has positive connotations. Their love may be carnal—but in this world, at this time, and in this place, it is a meaningful, religious act. In this context, the church suggests the traditional implications of a refuge and haven;

it is here that Winston and Julia can talk of the past and can make love. If they are unknowingly watched even in this "dusty" tower, they are still dramatically more free than in the room above the antique shop, where the telescreen camera looks through the picture of the church on the wall. Eros is preferable to agape when God is Big Brother, or, as we shall shortly see, "God is Power."

The meeting at O'Brien's home introduces a more far-reaching incorporation of religion into the plot. The scene between Winston, Julia, and O'Brien is based on a combination of religious rituals as O'Brien supposedly receives Winston and Julia into the Brotherhood. O'Brien first offers Winston and Julia some wine (which they do not recognize), served by O'Brien's oriental, altar-boy-like servant. O'Brien follows this by questioning Winston and Julia in a "routine, a sort of catechism, most of whose answers were known to him already."

> "You are prepared to give your lives?"
> "Yes."
> "You are prepared to commit murder?"
> "Yes."
> "To commit acts of sabotage which may cause the death of hundreds of innocent people?"
> "Yes."
> "To betray your country to foreign powers?"
> "Yes." (p. 173)

But the catechism ends when first Julia and then Winston refuse to agree to separate and never see each other again if the Brotherhood were to demand it. This love of man is the final sin which must be cleansed from Winston's soul in Room 101. O'Brien arranges to send Winston "a copy of the book," and Winston notices that O'Brien "seemed to pronounce the words as though they were in italics" (p. 178). In this world, the Bible is transformed into Emmanuel Goldstein's *The Theory and Practice of Oligarchical Collectivism.* The scene ends on a note of irony: O'Brien gives Winston and Julia a wafer—to kill the smell of wine so the elevator attendants will not notice. From catechism to communion, Winston and Julia are incorporated into the spiritual body of Big Brother. Following this scene, the religious overtones of Part Three are logical: The cleansing of Winston's soul by O'Brien, a "priest of power," in the secular Hell of the Ministry of Love is only the "reintegration" of the wayward lamb back into the flock.[28]

The implications of the religious metaphors Orwell uses touch other significant aspects of both plot and theme. Winston reads *The Theory and Practice of Oligarchical Collectivism* as he lies in bed beside the dozing Julia. In what at first seems a meaningless detail, after Winston has read about a paragraph of the opening of the book, "suddenly, as one sometimes does of a book of which one knows that one will ultimately read and reread every word," he opened "it at a different place and found himself at the third chapter" (pp. 185–186). Winston reads the third chapter, which gives much of the "historical" background of the division of the world into opposing factions. He then returns to the opening chapter, which is primarily theoretical and describes the rationale by which the Party exists. This chapter, in short, describes how the world of *1984* is; Winston begins to read the explanation of the motivations for all this inexplicable tyranny.

> But there is one question which until this moment we have almost ignored. It is: *why* should human equality be averted? Supposing that the mechanics of the process have been rightly described, what is the motive for this huge, accurately planned effort to freeze history at a particular moment of time?
>
> Here we reach the central secret. As we have seen, the mystique of the Party, and above all of the Inner Party, depends upon *doublethink*. But deeper than this lies the original motive, the never-questioned instinct that first led to the seizure of power and brought doublethink, the Thought Police, continuous warfare, and all the other necessary paraphernalia into existence afterwards. This motive really consists. . . . (p. 218)

Winston falls asleep, now understanding *how* but not yet

understanding *why*. He falls asleep murmuring "sanity is not statistical," but the sum of two and two is soon to deny that. The next morning Winston and Julia are taken prisoner.

The unanswered question about motivation is resolved in the Ministry of Love, where O'Brien finally answers Winston's query.[29] The answer is summed up in the apothegm "God is Power." This new religion, of which O'Brien is a "priest of power," can exist in the terms of deity because it ignores the error of self-rationalization made by tyrannies in the past. Oceania does not make martyrs; it makes converts. It does not allow a man to die a rebel; it "makes the brain perfect"—before it is blown out. In short, "Power is not a means; it is an end" (p. 266). The system which needs no self-justification can dispense with ideology;[30] with no need to objectify its purposes it can even alter reality to suit changing goals —though, ironically, the goal is constant: the perpetuation of power. Reality is what the Party *today* determines it to be; history is relative; the sun is no longer the center of the universe; the human spirit, which Winston solitarily asserts, ends in a gin-streaked, tearful prayer: ". . . his soul was white as snow. . . . He had won the victory over himself. He loved Big Brother" (p. 300).

A word must be said about the apparent alternatives to this total despair. A recurring phrase throughout the novel is "if there is hope, it lies in the proles." In the plot the hope which the proles represent seems to exist primarily in their existence outside the detailed control to which, for example, Winston is subject. They maintain a link with custom and language; sensual pleasures and the possession of "useless" items are possible for them; instinctual behavior has not vanished from their culture. In terms of Orwell's vaunted socialism and egalitarianism, it is tempting to see the proles as a mode of hope in this otherwise total tyranny.[31] In terms of the political theory presented in the book, such hope is denied. In Goldstein's book (written, of course, by the collective Party, including O'Brien, who vouches for the truth of its "description"), we learn that from the Proletarians nothing is to be feared. Left to themselves, they will continue from generation to generation and century to century, working, breeding, and dying, not only without any impulse to rebel, but without the power of grasping that the world could be other than what it is. (p. 211)

In a world in which power is all-important, the proles do not have the ability to conceptualize change, much less the power to bring about change.

The apparent hope that the proles bear is more subtly denied by the metaphors Orwell employs to describe them. Winston thinks about the proles, believing that only they can be the means to overthrow the Party—someday.

Even if the legendary Brotherhood existed, as just possibly it might, it was inconceivable that its members could ever assemble in larger numbers than twos and threes. Rebellion meant a look in the eyes, an inflection of the voice; at the most, an occasional whispered word. But the proles, if only they could somehow become conscious of their own strength, would have no need to conspire. They needed only to rise up and shake themselves like a horse shaking off flies. (pp. 69–70)

The linking of animal imagery with the proles recurs consistently.

In reality very little was known about the proles. It was not necessary to know much. So long as they continued to work and breed, their other activities were without importance. Left to themselves, like cattle turned loose upon the plains of Argentina, they had reverted to a style of life that appeared to be natural to them, a sort of ancestral pattern. (p. 71)

The continued equation of the proles with animals vitiates the rhetorical hope that Winston invests in them. The fate of brutish, stupid animal power has been made only too clear by *Animal Farm*. In a sense, the proles of *1984* are merely the helpless animals of *Animal Farm* transposed to a more efficient tyranny. One of the many equations running through *1984* is "orthodoxy is unconsciousness"; the proles may exist outside of the overt control of the state, but their unconsciousness marks them as Oceania's most loyal "members."

The apotheosis of admittedly evil, naked power existing for and of itself is an ultimate extension of the domination of politics over the individual. This is the point Irving Howe is making when he calls *1984* "the end of the line."

> A movement in which terror and irrationality play so great a role may finally have no goal beyond terror and irrationality; to search for an ultimate end that can be significantly related to its immediate activity may itself be a rationalist fallacy.[32]

The end of human reason may be the ultimate indignity that man can suffer. But the fabric of the novel suggests that Orwell's concern is with means and not ends. If power is an end in itself, the essential means to the attainment of that power is the same concept that Orwell has articulated, in varying contexts and with differing implications, since his first book and which had dominated his thoughts since his experiences in the Spanish Civil War—the corruption of language.

Too many details of the novel are unexplained if the theme of language corrupted and corrupting is slighted. For even O'Brien's view of the "perfected" world is couched in terms of the future: The world the Party is creating is a world that "will" happen:

> No one dares trust a wife or a child or a friend any longer. But in the future there will be no wives and no friends. Children will be taken from their mothers at birth, as one takes eggs from a hen. The sex instinct will be eradicated. Procreation will be an annual formality like the renewal of a ration card. We shall abolish the orgasm. Our neurologists are at work upon it now. There will be no loyalty, except loyalty toward the Party. There will be no love, except the love of Big Brother. There will be no laughter,

except the laugh of triumph over a defeated enemy. There will be no art, no literature, no science. When we are omnipotent we shall have no more need of science. (p. 270)

O'Brien admits, in passing, that the Party is not yet omnipotent. In terms of control over the deviant, it is, for all practical purposes, all-powerful; but the power is not yet absolute, and the tense and terms which describe the absolutism are radically utopian. However, the control of language is seen in more definite, empirical realizations; it is even possible to date it. Winston is talking to Syme, whose work in the "Research Department" is the continuous rewriting of the Newspeak dictionary.

> "The Eleventh Edition is the definitive edition," he said. "We're getting the language into its final shape—the shape it's going to have when nobody speaks anything else. When we've finished with it, people like you will have to learn it all over again. You think, I dare say, that our chief job is inventing new words. But not a bit of it! We're destroying words—scores of them, hundreds of them, every day. We're cutting the language down to the bone. The Eleventh Edition won't contain a single word that will become obsolete before the year 2050."[33]

Like so many other norms which are reversed in the world of *1984*, the dictionary becomes a means to narrow language, a way to diminish the range of vocabulary. The dictionary predicts and thus determines the choices of speech—and thus thought—and thus action—available to the inhabitants of Oceania. For language is the means by which men move out of their isolation; it is the means by which they particularize their concept of self, distinguishing it from another self—in the world of *1984*, the state's self. In George Steiner's words, it is in language that man's "identity and historical presence are uniquely explicit. It is language that severs man from the deterministic signal codes, from the inarticulacies, from the silences that inhabit the greater part of being."[34] The loss of choice in language leads to the loss of particularization, and this leads to unconsciousness. Syme again speaks to Winston.

> "Don't you see that the whole aim of Newspeak is to narrow the range of thought? In the end we shall make thought-crime literally impossible, because there will be no words in which to express it. Every concept that can ever be needed will be expressed by exactly one word with its meaning rigidly defined and all its subsidiary meanings rubbed out and forgotten. Already, in the Eleventh Edition, we're not far from that point. But the process will still be continuing long after you and I are dead. Every year fewer and fewer words, and the range of consciousness always a little smaller. Even now, of course, there's no reason or excuse for committing thought-crime. It's merely a question of self-discipline, reality control. But in the end there won't by any need even for that. The Revolution will be complete when the language is perfect. . . . By the year 2050, at the very latest, not a single human being will be alive who could understand such a conversation as we are having now.
>
> .   .   .   .
>
> The whole climate of thought will be different. In fact there will be no thought, as we understand it now. Orthodoxy means not thinking—not needing to think. Orthodoxy is unconsciousness." (pp. 53–54)

The world which O'Brien is able only to predict can be casually assumed and fixed by a minor clerk, one whose fate is to himself vanish: "Syme had ceased to exist; he had never existed" (p. 148). In a world where the past is always mutable in the constant alteration of language, existence is indeed indeterminable.

> . . . though the past is alterable, it never has been altered in any specific instance. For when it has been recreated in whatever shape is needed at the moment, then this new version is the past, and no different past can ever have existed. (pp. 214–215)

The horrors of the physical tortures, the total lack of privacy, the malevolent secularization of concepts of eternity, the absolute tyranny of the state—all these are ultimate in *1984*. Nevertheless they seem to me subsidiary to the more comprehensive and contemporary mode of oppression that vitally informs *1984*. The book is, for all its coherence of structure, thematically incomplete without the Appendix. The horror of Winston's fate is not that he betrayed his "inner heart" in asserting his love of his selfhood over his love of Julia; nor is the absolute control of the state over the individual, through physical torture and death or consummate brainwashing, the worst terror that the human being can face. "The end of the line" in *1984* is the loss of consciousness—and Orwell specifically defines this as a result of the failure of language. Most disturbing, after all the monstrousness the book implies for the human condition, is that "The Principles of Newspeak" are described in the *past* tense. If we believe Orwell, we are past 1984 and closing in on 2050.

VIII

CONCLUSION

It is tempting at this point to rank Orwell among the
great novelists of the twentieth century. This, I believe,
would be misleading and invalid. Even the most sympathetic reader of Orwell's six novels—and I am one—cannot
in fairness rate him with Lawrence, Conrad, or James. But I
do think that Orwell's work deserves a much higher esteem
than it has generally received. If comparisons are meaningful,
I would suggest that Orwell's novels earn him a position
comparable to the position of such a well-regarded novelist
as E. M. Forster. This may be a relevant comparison: I would
hold that Orwell's first novel, Burmese Days, does not suffer
greatly in comparison with Forster's last, A Passage to India.
The novels share not only a similar background but a common theme—the tenuousness of human community. And if
Forster has maintained his considerable reputation largely on
the basis of two or three fine novels (Howards End, A Passage to India, perhaps Where Angels Fear to Tread), Orwell
should in justice have such a rating on the basis of Burmese
Days, Animal Farm, and 1984. If Burmese Days is a fine
novel, certainly Animal Farm is a classic of its own kind, a
rare accomplishment within a long-standing tradition, a book

that succeeds despite the inherent dangers of the *roman à clef*
and of allegorization. And we have seen that *1984* is a
finely constructed work of fiction as well as a significant political statement. For politics is, it must be admitted, an integral
part of Orwell's art. One can asseverate—as I have done—the
necessity of considering his novels as novels. But, in truth, textual analysis is only a first step for fully appreciating Orwell.

His career demonstrates in an unmatched way a significant
phenomenon of our literature: the impact of politics on the
artistic imagination. This occurrence is visible in writers as
disparate as Malraux and Koestler, Dos Passos and Richard
Wright, Norman Mailer and Ezra Pound. And despite cultural predispositions to the contrary, it is impossible to say
that this impact has been in any measurable way harmful to
such writers. Indeed, the supposed sullying muse of politics—
such an assumption is long-standing and present even in this
highly politicized time—probably has made a major contribution to the achievements of, for example, the superb crafts-
manship of Dos Passos, the raw power of Wright, the genius
of Pound. But it is unarguable that at the same time politics
has often led the artist toward disenchantment and distrust
of ideologies and systems or, as is common, to a retreat from
the horrors of politics to other forms, new systems in which
to invest belief. Wright and Hemingway demonstrate clearly
enough the retreat from the commitment to ideology to that
of self; Malraux and Koestler show the movement from
engagement in politics to preoccupation with other "isms"—
the commitment to art, philosophy, psychology. We assent
to such a development in the career of an artist as understandable and natural. The true artist, sensitive to human
nuance, must inevitably deny the corruptiveness of ideology,
the sham of practical politics. Aware of Stendahl's famous
pistol-shot, the artist, like the critic, is aware that politics
taints art and artist.

The assumption is common: Politics is seldom fit subject
for the novel. At worst, the novel becomes a vehicle for
propaganda; at best, the assimilation of political action or

ideas into the fictive world is difficult, if not impossible. On the first charge, there can only be agreement, if the example in mind is the kind of mindless proletarian novel of the 1930's in the United States: made to order, slavishly class-oriented, devoid of imagination or life. But for the "prize-winning" *Marching! Marching!* there is a *Nostromo*; for any novel written to conform to *New Masses* criteria there is *Darkness at Noon*; for Clara Weatherwax there is Ignazio Silone. This is not to suggest that the genre of the political novel—if in fact it merits such a classification—is not filled with dross and second-rate stuff. But the field is sufficiently rich to contradict the notion that somehow politics is necessarily uncongenial and even destructive material for literature. Fiction is more substantial and hardy than many will allow. Yet such belief persists. One of our finest critics, sensitive to the social service of literature and by no means dogmatic about "proper" kinds of fiction, can nevertheless reiterate most recently the commonplace notion that somehow art is—and should be—separate from immediacy, must in some way transcend the particular, avoid partisanship—or be denied artistic immortality in some mystical but unspecified way:

> If one proposes that it is the business or nature of literature to engage in dissent (or, for that matter, assent), one is trying to make it over into journalism, propaganda, topical pleading. If he succeeded in persuading a writer that this was his mission, he would make it ever so much harder for the writer to get out of his own decade into the company of the great. For it is the business of the writer, and the essence of literature, not to dissent or assent, but, as I said earlier, to discover and frame artistically a vision of reality.[1]

The idea endures. But if it is common, it is not necessarily valid. And even if it were valid—and I think it is not—Orwell would surely be the clear exception to the pattern. He shows how politics, its effect, its study, its depths and heights, can enrich a sensibility, can mature and educate a writer. His entire artistic life reveals the unifying thread of politics. The growth of political apprehensions and their incorporation into a fictional world is the most significant aspect in his development. The fact of politics is present in his first three novels, but the political specifics—colonialism, poverty, organized religion—are thematically limited and parochial. However, Orwell's last three works of fiction reveal a different political vision and a more successful fusion of the political insights into the fictional form. The minor tyrannies which the individual faced and could at least combat if not conquer in the early novels have in the later ones been expanded into a totalitarianism that is absolute and terrible in its implications for the individual and for society. Orwell's most profound insight envisions an absolute totalitarianism which precludes individuality in society. Having experienced the futility of ideological commitment in Spain, having recognized the gap between pronouncements of social amelioration and their inoperability in the industrial towns of England, having finally come to the realization that power, the anathema of liberalism, has become an end in itself, Orwell announces that man's choices are gone from the world. If John Flory was faced with horrid social and moral alternatives, he had at least the option of suicide, in its destruction the last assertion of self; Winston Smith does not have even that.

Irving Howe has well demonstrated the movement from "social" novel to "political" novel (a movement which Orwell himself seems to recapitulate), a phenomenon in which nineteenth-century beginnings have led to the achievements of Conrad, James, Malraux, and others. Howe suggests that the crucial distinction between the two genres is to be found in the conception of society, in the growth of the questioning of the assumptions which underlie community; in Howe's words, in the political novel the very *idea* of society is called into account. But the twentieth century has proven that there are different kinds of tyranny to be feared, varying kinds of societies to apprehend. The political worlds of Aldous Huxley and Henry James are, I think, equally called to account, equally fearful; but they have different bases. James' continuing political horror was anarchism; Huxley's bogey of progress was science. But Orwell's insights were different yet. In his world, the means by which such absolute control is to be maintained over the individual is the control of language. For we see in the novels a concern with language which far transcends the aphorisms and strictures of his essays. The role played by language grows from a relatively small one in *Burmese Days*, where it is a vehicle of human communication and thus human intercourse and love, through satiric attacks on advertising, a readily available representative of the corruption of language in *Keep the Aspidistra Flying*, to the profoundly shattering conception of the absolute control of man's private self by the control of his language in *1984*. In the world of *1984*, Winston Smith's political isolation and human loneliness follow parallel courses, and in the end Winston is no longer socially isolated nor humanly alone; but he has lost his selfhood as he is incorporated back into the healthy body politic and becomes part of the totalitarian state. He *believes* the contradictions of that society's language; he ceases to be a rational human when he knows that "Freedom is Slavery," that two and two equal five. The façade of hope in the essays, implicit in the reasonableness of the tone and overt in many statements, is lost in the developing perceptions of the novels; no "plant" pushes blindly to the light in the fiction to suggest the eventual rebirth of humane possibilities. In the final novels, the dominant light is the purifying horror of Room 101.

The central impetus of his mature apprehensions of the uses of language in modern society is tersely suggested in Orwell's retrospective essay, "Why I Write" (1946): "The Spanish War and other events in 1936–7 turned the scale and thereafter I knew where I stood." It was his personal involvement in the Spanish Civil War and then the implications of the journalistic distortions of fact, which he had seen in Spain and expressed in *Homage to Catalonia*, that marked the turning point in his development. I am wary of claiming too much for the effect of this war on modern literature, but

at least on Orwell the effect is demonstrable. Certain attitudes, certain kinds of characters, certain basic values remain
constant in Orwell's career from start to finish. But there is
no escaping the fact that he is a very different writer after
Spain. The change is in his conception of the relation of man
to his community; after Spain, Orwell recognizes a new kind
of society. The resolutions of Keep the Aspidistra Flying and
1984 are essentially the same: Following rebellion, the protagonist comes to terms with his society. But following the les-
sons of Spain, the society is a completely different thing, the
overtones far more tragic, and the implications for the human
spirit far more dire.

Orwell's political and literary insights are not limited to
this one terrible conflict. In his writings we see many of the
significant intellectual perceptions of our culture. To read
Orwell is to realize the meaning of Ortega y Gasset's indict-
ment of twentieth-century liberalism. For all the works of
Orwell reiterate the belief that modern liberalism misunder-
stands the "fierce nature of the state" and overlooks the
tyranny that any state brings to any one individual. To read
Animal Farm is to experience in the deceptive dress and tone
of the beast fable-fairy tale the brutalizing effect on the victim of violence and degradation, which has been shown by
people as various as D. H. Lawrence and Bruno Bettleheim.
Both assailant and victim are degraded by the fact of violence, and we see this phenomenon in Orwell's writing from
the Club members of Burmese Days, who become appropriate beasts in their jungle worlds because of their brutal behavior toward others, to the breathtaking scene in which
Winston Smith embraces his torturer, O'Brien. Concepts
which now seem so common to any study of modern literature—self, alienation, deracination, violence—must inevitably
recur in a sympathetic consideration of Orwell's fiction.

I hope that this study suggests in a preliminary way facts
which will alter Orwell's place in literary history, a place
which should be among the novelists, not among the pamphleteers. At the very least, he should be seen as one of the

foremost political novelists of a century in which the political novel is a significant force. But no matter where his literary accomplishments are finally ranked, his personal place in the history of our culture is assured by the force of the values he asserts. I suspect that the most important gain, because the most lasting, that we derive from reading Orwell is our knowledge of his own personal ideas, feelings, and responses to our world. Whether or not these make subject matter for his novels, we do gain from them an image of their author as a man of remarkable virtues. It is paradoxical that the greatest impression one gets from extensive reading in Orwell is a sense of the "eternal verities," an old-fashioned humanism in the writer of the most famous twentieth-century vision of man's future. Any final judgment turns to the epithets which I disdained at the outset of this study: "decency," "virtuous." But perhaps this kind of personal force is salutary and even necessary in an age in which ideology is suspect, the power of personal action in doubt, and man's integrity annihilated by politics. In the man who foresaw these phenomena clearly, we see what we hope is their counter—the force of a personality that can convincingly assert that the individual is still the measure of value. And nothing reveals the force of this individual more clearly or more powerfully than the artistry of his works.

Notes

I. BURMESE DAYS

[1] John Atkins, *George Orwell* (New York, 1954), p. 84.

[2] *Burmese Days* (New York, 1950), p. 17. Subsequent references are to this edition and are in the text.

[3] Frederick R. Karl, *A Reader's Guide to the Contemporary English Novel* (New York, 1962), p. 155.

[4] The term anticipates a similar episode in *1984*. There, Winston Smith is forced to do the "Physical Jerks" by the omnipotent and omnipresent telescreen. Perhaps the only real differences between the tyrannical societies of Kyauktada and Oceania are the degree of compulsion and the number of options open to the inhabitants.

[5] Cf. "Shooting an Elephant" (1936).

[6] P. 57. This is the scene where Flory is bathing in the clear water. A green pigeon comes down onto a branch just above the pool: "The pigeon rocked itself backwards and forwards on the bough, swelling out its breast feathers and laying its coralline beak upon them. A pang went through Flory. Alone, alone, the bitterness of being alone! So often like this, in lonely places in the forest, he would come upon something —bird, flower, tree—beautiful beyond words, if there had been a soul with whom to share it." Not the least of the pangs that Flory suffers here is frustration stimulated by the bird's sexual dance.

[7] In a nice touch, Elizabeth wears tortoise-shell rimmed glasses; at the end of the novel, the two marry, as, symbolically, they almost must.

[8] The dog image is not exclusive to Flory. At one point, Veraswami, in his tearful gratitude, has eyes which "beamed upon Flory like the liquid eyes of a dog" (p. 150). And just a few pages later, Ma Hla May accuses Flory of driving her from his "door like a dog" (p. 154). The common denominator is servitude.

[9] The opening paragraph of the book concludes with the image of "a few vultures" circling "without the quiver of a wing" (p. 5). The image recurs *passim*. Other images foreshadowing death are present throughout. At one point Flory and his servant carefully picked leeches from Flo's coat—in a scene following the dramatic representation of some of Flory's human parasites.

[10] See George Woodcock, *The Crystal Spirit: A Study of George Orwell* (Boston, 1966), p. 95. While Mr. Woodcock's treatment of *Burmese Days* is of necessity less detailed than is my study, I am pleased that he and I agree on most matters. The important fact, however, is that he treats the book as an imaginative artifice and not as a tract, contrary to most of Orwell's critics.

[11] After the riot, the Club garden looks "as though a herd of bison had stampeded across it" (p. 255). Flory has put another beast to rout.

[12] The idea recurs throughout Orwell's writings. Religious structures and metaphors are consistently used in negative or ironic contexts to illustrate the meaninglessness of organized religion in the modern age.

[13] In Edmund Wilson, *The Wound and the Bow* (London, 1961), pp. 244–264.

[14] Wilson, p. 264.

[15] "Why I Write," in *Collected Essays* (London, 1961), p. 421.

II. A CLERGYMAN'S DAUGHTER

[1] Christopher Hollis, *A Study of George Orwell: The Man and His Works* (London, 1956), p. 58.

[2] Frank W. Wadsworth, "Orwell As A Novelist: The Early Work," *University of Kansas City Review*, XXII, ii (Winter, 1955), 97.

[3] John Atkins, *George Orwell* (New York, 1954), p. 84.

[4] Laurence Brander, *George Orwell* (London, 1954), p. 92.

[5] *A Clergyman's Daughter* (New York, n.d.), p. 250. Subsequent references are to this edition and are in the text.

[6] Hollis, p. 58. Hollis' term is technically incorrect. Dorothy loses her memory, not her power to speak or understand

speech. Richard J. Voorhees is almost unique in thinking that Dorothy's amnesia has cause. *The Paradox of George Orwell* (Lafayette, Indiana, 1961), p. 46.

[7] "Lear, Tolstoy and the Fool," in *Collected Essays* (London, 1961), p. 413.

[8] It is not the Anglican Church *itself* that is the target of Orwell's satire; it is any organized religion. The neighboring town of Millborough has a competing Roman Catholic church: There, "they were said to have a parrot which they were teaching to say 'Extra eccelsiam nulla salus'" (p. 25).

[9] A. E. Dyson, *The Crazy Fabric: Essays in Irony* (London, 1965), p. 204.

[10] With ". . . meanly decent streets, all so indistinguishably alike, with their ranks of semi-detached houses, their privet and laurel hedges and plots of ailing shrubs at the crossroads" (p. 214), Southbridge anticipates the modern Lower Binfield of *Coming Up For Air*.

[11] P. 316. The "ant-heaps of steel and concrete" utopia seems to be the earliest foreshadowing in Orwell's writings of the world of *1984*.

[12] An alternative reading of the conclusion is to see Orwell as being ironic. Dorothy's contemplation of the glue-pot could be construed as a prevision of Winston Smith's final, reverent gaze upon the picture of Big Brother. Emanuel Edrich seems to hold this view: "Thus, as Orwell paints it, if present trends continue, the man (or woman) of the middle class has nothing to look forward to whether he protests or conforms" ("George Orwell and the Satire in Horror," *Texas Studies in Literature and Language*, IV, i [Spring, 1962], 104). This seems to me a possible reading—but more a result of conceptions of what we *want* to have Orwell say. There is no indication elsewhere that Orwell is ironic in the final attitude toward Dorothy's fate. In the passage cited above, the authorial voice intrudes to make plain that this is a lesson which will be learned—and, implicity, *should* be learned—ultimately.

[13] The choice for life may be seen as, in this respect, Orwell's reaction to his own portrayal of Flory's suicide in *Burmese Days*. Wadsworth says this novel is more pessimistic than was *Burmese Days* in sending Dorothy "back to a living

death" and rejecting the "unreal solution of suicide" (p. 98). I do not think Orwell felt at this point that to live—even a miserable life—is more "pessimistic" than to die. And surely the tone of *A Clergyman's Daughter* is far lighter, far less hopeless than that of *Burmese Days*.

[14] Hollis, pp. 59, 71–72.

III. KEEP THE ASPIDISTRA FLYING

[1] Christopher Hollis, *A Study of George Orwell: The Man and His Works* (London, 1956), p. 71.

[2] Laurence Brander, *George Orwell* (London, 1954), p. 107.

[3] John Mander, *The Writer and Commitment* (London, 1961), p. 74.

[4] Hollis, p. 71.

[5] Stephen Greenblatt, *Three Modern Satirists: Waugh, Orwell and Huxley* (New Haven, 1965), pp. 53, 56.

[6] Wyndham Lewis, "Orwell, or Two and Two Make Four," in *The Writer and the Absolute* (London, 1952), p. 176. Only Richard Voorhees seems to remark Orwell's purposes: "The point that Orwell is making . . . is that Gordon is, until the very end of the book, a fool." (*The Paradox of George Orwell* [Lafayette, Indiana, 1961], p. 34).

[7] Greenblatt, p. 54.

[8] "Reflections on Gandhi," in *Shooting an Elephant and Other Essays* (New York, 1950), p. 98.

[9] *Keep the Aspidistra Flying* (New York, 1956), p. 14. Subsequent references are to this, the first American edition, and are in the text.

[10] The literary allusion in the passage above is part of a pattern throughout the novel. Gordon, as a member of the literati, continually quotes poetry: e.g., Marvell, Keats, Wyatt. At times the references provide a nice irony: when the sexually frustrated Gordon is walking the streets of London, he thinks "They flee from me that sometime did me seek" (p. 72). This fits in well in the creation of Gordon's character; he is a poet—of sorts. This technique is less appropriately used when Rosemary, Gordon's girl, conscious of her age, muses that "Time's wingèd chariot was hurrying near" (p. 214). There

is little evidence in the novel to suggest that kind of reference likely in Rosemary. But this scarcely bothers the reader.

[11] P. 126. In *1984*, Winston and Julia make a similar journey to the countryside, for the occasion of their first love-making. The situation is described in almost the same terms: Winston feels the burden of his London environment as alien in nature; he also feels "etiolated."

[12] P. 151. The image is reminiscent of Ezra Pound's famous "Canto XLV," "With Usura." "Usura . . . hath brought palsey to the bed, lyeth/between the young bride and her bridegroom/CONTRA NATURUM." (*The Cantos of Ezra Pound* [New York, 1948], p. 24.) The parallel is suggestive. Obviously, Pound and Orwell are politically poles apart, yet, as so often seems the case in political extremism, there are many affinities between the two. Though it is Gordon here who sees politics and/or economics as intervening against the natural sexual act, Orwell also shares this belief, even though he is generally ironic toward Gordon's attitudes in this book. In *The Road to Wigan Pier*, Orwell refutes the idea that the unemployed should not get married: ". . . losing your job does not mean that you cease to be a human being" (London, 1937, p. 88.). Perhaps a more significant similarity in thought of these two very different men is their common concern with the corruption of language—a concern which both locate in the political world.

[13] Orwell's attitudes toward ineffectual, theoretical socialism are suggested in the person of Ravelston. He is a socialist, but is offended by any contact with the lower classes; he publishes a radical magazine, but the image of its title on his door suggests only comic irony:

P.W.H. RAVELSTON

ANTICHRIST

[14] In Frederick Karl's words, ". . . his difficulties seem to emanate as much from what he is as from the social ills he suffers." (*A Reader's Guide to the Contemporary English Novel* [New York, 1962], p. 162.)

[15] P. 202. This is perhaps a prevision of the Pornosec department in the Ministry of Truth of *1984*, which turns out cheap pornography for the proles.

[16] P. 203. This kind of "vertical" metaphor recurs in Or-

well's writings. In *Down and Out in Paris and London*, Orwell portrays his own movement "down" from conventional social norms; in *Coming Up For Air*, the hero, as we shall see, is caught between conflicting pulls—*down*, into the "muck" of society, or *up*, into the freedom of clear air—which, ironically, turns out to be not so pure.

IV. HOMAGE TO CATALONIA

[1] *Homage to Catalonia* (New York, 1952), p. 4. Subsequent references are to this edition and are in the text.

[2] There have been several recent books concerning the writer and/or intellectual and the Spanish Civil War. Perhaps the best are John M. Muste's *Say That We Saw Spain Die* (Seattle, 1966) and Hugh D. Ford's *A Poets' War: British Poets and the Spanish Civil War* (Philadelphia, 1965). Also valuable is Frederick R. Benson's *Writers in Arms: The Literary Impact of the Spanish Civil War* (New York, 1967). Stanley Weintraub's *The Last Great Cause: The Intellectuals and the Spanish Civil War* (New York, 1968) has a lamentably weak chapter on *Homage to Catalonia*, but is full of names, facts, anecdotes.

[3] This ironic attitude toward the various parties' initials was apparently common. Cf. Hemingway's *For Whom the Bell Tolls*, where the cynical General Karkov disdains the P.O.U.M. rebellion: "The P.O.U.M. It is like the name. Not serious. They should have called it the M.U.M.P.S. or the M.E.A.S.L.E.S. But no, the measles is much more dangerous" (New York, 1940, p. 247).

[4] *A Clergyman's Daughter* (New York, n.d.), p. 144.

[5] P. 51. The question of communist motives in the war is still much debated. I am here not so much concerned with the truth of such charges as with the reasons for Orwell's willingness to believe them. An interesting discussion of the question of the writer as dupe in Spain is in *A Poets' War*, pp. 254–257. One major point Ford makes is that to be duped was perhaps inevitable: How could the involved person, writer or otherwise, possibly have the means, much less the foresight, to see through the confusion, deception, and chaos of this struggle? Orwell's views in *Homage*, written imme-

diately following his return from Spain, are remarkably perspicacious by any standard.

6 In *Collected Essays* (London, 1961), p. 186—hereafter cited as "Looking Back."

7 "Looking Back," p. 195.

8 "Looking Back," p. 196.

9 "Looking Back," p. 197.

10 New York, 1961, p. 190.

11 A political-psychological explanation is also possible. Orwell's immediate and unexpected enlistment into the Republican militia may be seen as an attempt to make the fullest possible commitment to belief—and to be wounded confirms such commitment. As Francis Hope says of Spain, "death in battle is a solider guarantee of sincerity than the most impeccable working-class pedigree." *The Review*, XI–XII (n.d.), 6.

12 Laurence Brander, *George Orwell* (London, 1954), p. 128.

13 Richard Rees, *George Orwell: Fugitive From the Camp of Victory* (London, 1961), p. 65.

14 Individual reactions to the horrors of the war naturally vary. Still, Orwell's dominant tone is somewhat rare. For discussions of other writers' reactions see Ford's *A Poets' War* (especially pp. 101–127) and Muste's *Say That We Saw Spain Die* (the chapter called "Bullets Hurt, Corpses Stink," pp. 120–152).

15 Frederick J. Hoffman, *The Mortal No* (Princeton, 1964), p. 121 *et passim*. Professor Hoffman traces this image throughout modern literature.

16 E.g., "To the Spanish people, at any rate in Catalonia and Aragon, the Church was a racket pure and simple" (p. 81).

17 Only recently has there been much discussion of the effect of this war on the artists. See especially *A Poets' War*, pp. 85–97 (the chapter entitled "Politics and Literature") and *Writers in Arms*, pp. 51–87 ("Political Commitment and the Writer"). The subject has yet to be exhausted, however. And while the larger and more interesting esthetic problem, the relationship of art to politics, has been the subject of countless discussions, it seems to me the problem has not yet been adequately, sympathetically, or unbiasedly ap-

proached. The most exciting discussion may well be Trotsky's *Literature and Revolution*. A recent and interesting book is John R. Harrison's *The Reactionaries: A Study of the Anti-Democratic Intelligensia* (New York, 1967).

V. COMING UP FOR AIR

[1] John Mander, *The Writer and Commitment* (London, 1961), p. 73. This attitude has much currency. See, for example, Harold J. Harris, "Orwell's Essays and *1984*," *Twentieth Century Literature*, IV, iv (January, 1959), 154–161.

[2] Christopher Hollis, *A Study of George Orwell: The Man and His Works* (London, 1956), p. 112.

[3] George Woodcock, *The Crystal Spirit* (Boston, 1966), p. 181. For myself, I am more and more convinced that there are no valid "rules" in art. Either things work or they don't.

[4] Frank W. Wadsworth, "Orwell as Novelist—The Middle Period," *University of Kansas City Review*, XXII, iii (Spring, 1956), 194.

[5] Laurence Brander, *George Orwell* (London, 1954), pp. 151–152.

[6] Richard Rees, *George Orwell: Fugitive From the Camp of Victory* (London, 1961), p. 80.

[7] Mander, p. 106.

[8] "The Art of Fiction" in *Henry James: Selected Fiction*, ed. Leon Edel (New York, 1953), p. 591.

[9] Wayne Booth, *The Rhetoric of Fiction* (Chicago, 1961), p. 17.

[10] Booth, p. 19.

[11] ". . . the art of fiction does not begin until the novelist thinks of his story to be *shown*, to be exhibited so that it will tell itself." Percy Lubbock, *The Craft of Fiction* (New York, 1957), p. 62. Lubbock's italics.

[12] I follow Booth's definitions here: An "unreliable narrator" is one who does *not* speak or act in accordance with the norms of the work (which is to say, the implied author's norms); a reliable narrator is one who does. Booth, pp. 158–159.

[13] Stephen Spender, "A Short History of the Pers. Pron. 1st Sing. Nom." in *The Struggle of the Modern* (London, 1963), p. 140.

[14] Frederick J. Hoffman, *The Mortal No* (Princeton, New

Jersey, 1964). Just prior to this, Professor Hoffman discusses the use point of view has in the "non-involvement" of certain contemporary French novelists. The literature of the 1950's, even that featuring a first person narrative such as *The Stranger* and *Nausea*, features "a certain scrupulousness on the part of the narrator with respect to avoiding commitment of himself emotionally to the occasion" (p. 467). Obviously George Bowling is deeply committed to his occasion.

[15] Hoffman, p. 229.

[16] Brander, p. 156. There is manipulation of narrative time elsewhere, although there is no other use of flashback, which is what Brander apparently means. In one section of *A Clergyman's Daughter* time is significantly altered. In *1984*, Orwell expertly manipulates time for some effective dramatic suspense.

[17] *Coming Up For Air* (New York, 1950), p. 29. Subsequent references are to this edition and are in the text.

[18] Pp. 27–28. The rubber skin and the shape of the frankfurter also suggest the "rubber truncheons" which George frequently visualizes as an aspect of the impending future.

[19] Frederick R. Karl, *A Reader's Guide to the Contemporary English Novel* (New York, 1962), p. 155.

[20] Isaac Rosenfeld, "Decency and Death," in *An Age of Enormity* (Cleveland and New York, 1962), p. 254.

[21] "Charles Dickens," in *Collected Essays* (London, 1961), p. 48.

[22] "Arthur Koestler," in *Collected Essays*, p. 231.

[23] Leo Marx, *The Machine in the Garden* (New York, 1964), p. 364.

[24] Tom Hopkinson, *George Orwell*, Writers and Their Work Series, No. 39 (London, 1962), p. 25.

[25] Richard J. Voorhees, *The Paradox of George Orwell* (Lafayette, Indiana, 1961), p. 109.

[26] Rees, pp. 82, 84.

[27] Northrop Frye, *The Anatomy of Criticism* (Princeton, New Jersey, 1957), p. 43.

VI. ANIMAL FARM

[1] Christopher Hollis, *A Study of George Orwell: The Man and His Works* (London, 1956), p. 138.

[2] E.g., John Mander, *The Writer and Commitment* (Lon-

don, 1961), ". . . the novels must be considered marginal to his real achievement." (p. 76)

[3] Laurence Brander, *George Orwell* (London, 1954), p. 170.

[4] Hollis, p. 139. The publication history of *Animal Farm* is interesting. Orwell had finished the book early in 1944 and submitted it to four publishers who refused it on "the ground that at that time . . . it was not possible to print a book attacking a military ally." (Tom Hopkinson, *George Orwell*, Writers and Their Work Series, No. 39 [London, 1962], p. 28.) Relations between Russia and the allies deteriorated so quickly following the war that the book was—one imagines, gloatingly—published in 1945.

[5] There is, however, some evidence—though tenuous and circumstantial—to suggest that Orwell spent much more time writing *Animal Farm* than Hollis and others believe. Rayner Heppenstall quotes a letter to him from Orwell, dated April 11, 1940, in which in the course of discussing his farming, Orwell says, "I haven't touched my novel [for some time]." Heppenstall only asks, "What novel? *Coming Up For Air* was already out." (*Four Absentees* [London, 1960], p. 153.) However, the book in question may have in fact been *1984*. Joseph Slater cites a remark of Orwell's in 1940 that his work in progress was not a prophetic fantasy nor a political satire, but "a novel in three parts"—obviously *1984*. Unfortunately, Mr. Slater does not give the source of this quotation. "The Fictional Values of *1984*," in Rudolf Kirk and C. W. Main, eds., *Essays in Literary History: Presented to J. Milton French* (New Brunswick, New Jersey, 1961), p. 254.

[6] In *Collected Essays* (London, 1961), p. 426.

[7] "Why I Write," in *Collected Essays*, p. 426. Orwell's italics.

[8] Hopkinson, *George Orwell*, p. 34.

[9] John Wain, "George Orwell (II)," in *Essays on Literature and Ideas* (London, 1963), p. 201.

[10] Ellen Douglass Leyburn, "Animal Stories," in *Modern Satire*, ed. Alvin B. Kernan (New York, 1962), p. 215.

[11] I. A. Richards, *The Philosophy of Rhetoric* (New York, 1936), p. 100.

[12] A comparison with *Homage to Catalonia* is revealing. This enormously praised book sold only 900 copies between

1938, its publication date, and 1950, the year of Orwell's death; and it was not printed in the United States until 1952.

[13] Frederick R. Karl, *A Reader's Guide to the Contemporary English Novel* (New York, 1962), pp. 162–163. Karl says that the "final result is not so much an exposé of man's iniquity as the lesser conclusion that animals would react like men were they to be given the choices that men have." This seems to assume that the book is concerned with the moral and social options of animals.

[14] Hopkinson, *George Orwell*, p. 28.

[15] Tom Hopkinson, "Animal Farm," *World Review*, new series 16 (June, 1950), 54.

[16] Richard Rees, *George Orwell: Fugitive From the Camp of Victory* (London, 1961), p. 90.

[17] E.g., if Major represents Lenin, there is some difficulty. Lenin died in 1924, well after the revolution had occurred; yet in *Animal Farm*, Major dies prior to the animals' revolt. Moreover, Major seems to represent the prophet of animal equality and class revolution, obviously more in conformance with Marx. But if Major represents Marx, there is an even worse anachronism.

[18] A. E. Dyson, "Orwell: Irony as Prophecy," in *The Crazy Fabric: Essays in Irony* (London, 1965), p. 206.

[19] *Animal Farm* (New York, 1954), p. 3. Subsequent references are to this edition and are in the text.

[20] Irving Howe, *Politics and the Novel* (New York, 1957), p. 243.

[21] Hopkinson, *George Orwell*, p. 29.

[22] P. 27. It is noteworthy that these children never appear in the book: They obviously would enjoy a natural sympathy that would be contrary to the antipathy the humans receive in the fable.

[23] This is certainly one realization of *1984*. The source of this idea in Orwell's writing may be James Burnham's *The Managerial Revolution*, a major source of *1984*.

[24] Arthur Koestler, *The Invisible Writing* (New York, 1954), p. 67.

[25] In R. L. Bruckberger, *One Sky to Spare* (New York, 1952), quoted in Koestler, pp. 155–156.

[26] P. 75. Orwell makes an important distinction here. While

there is some mismanagement on the farm and a great deal of confiscation and hoarding by the pigs, it is primarily the severe winter that brings the farm into jeopardy. The socialistic system itself is not wrong, though it appears Orwell thinks it cannot survive in isolation.

[27] The violation of the commandments develops according to the degree of seriousness of the violation. The first to be altered is the fourth, which merely adds "with sheets" to the pronouncement, "No animal shall sleep in a bed." The final violation is, of course, to the seventh, "All animals are equal."

[28] Cf. "Looking Back on the Spanish War." "The struggle of the working class is like the growth of a plant. The plant is blind and stupid, but it knows enough to keep pushing upwards towards the light and it will do this in the face of endless discouragement." (In Collected Essays, p. 200.) The metaphor is suggestive: Here Orwell employs the same terms of organic growth that exist in other contexts in Animal Farm. However, it seems to me that Orwell comes to realize that the implications of the metaphor fail in human political contexts. The logical extension is the proles of 1984; but the "hope" that the proles represent is as delusive and feeble as is Boxer.

VII. 1984

[1] T. R. Fyvel, "A Writer's Life," World Review, new series 16 (June, 1950), 19.

[2] Tom Hopkinson, George Orwell (London, 1956), p. 13.

[3] Irving Howe, Politics and the Novel (New York, 1957), p. 236.

[4] Howe, p. 237.

[5] Richard J. Voorhees, The Paradox of George Orwell (Lafayette, Indiana, 1961), p. 60. Stephen Greenblatt (Three Modern Satirists: Waugh, Orwell and Huxley [New Haven, 1965]) agrees that this material is outside possible "integration" into the plot (p. 69).

[6] "Why I Write," in Collected Essays (London, 1961), p. 425.

[7] Wyndham Lewis, The Writer and the Absolute (London, 1952), p. 190.

[8] January 4, 1946. Reprinted as "Freedom and Happiness"

in *Orwell's Nineteen Eighty-Four: Text, Sources, Criticism*, ed. Irving Howe (New York, 1963), pp. 151–153—hereafter cited as *Orwell's 1984*.

[9] Isaac Deutscher, "*1984*—The Mysticism of Cruelty," in *Orwell's 1984*, pp. 196–203.

[10] "Freedom and Happiness," *Orwell's 1984*, p. 151.

[11] Frank W. Wadsworth, "Orwell's Later Work," *University of Kansas City Review*, XXII, iv (June, 1956), 287. The image occurs in *We*, trans. Gregory Zilboorg (New York, 1952), on p. 64.

[12] In *Orwell's 1984*, p. 151.

[13] The image apparently had some currency. It occurs in much the same context and with much the same intent in a far different kind of work, John Strachey's polemic, *Literature and Dialectical Materialism* (New York, 1934), pp. 10–11.

[14] Ian Willison is most perceptive to this point. He suggests Orwell was revitalizing a mode of fiction absent from Conrad to Koestler, that is, political fiction. This "mode assumes the existence of an autonomous 'public world'" which alone "establishes the norms for judging 'what is the case' and what, therefore, is a 'fitting' opening and conclusion for the episode treated in the novel." He goes on to argue that this substitution of, in effect, a political *system* for a character or other conventional aspect of creating tension is Orwell's "contribution to the craft of fiction" ("Orwell's Good Bad Books," *Twentieth Century*, CLVII, 938 [April, 1955], 354–366). The only suggestion of Willison's with which I disagree is that this kind of writing may lead to the end of the distinction between fiction and nonfiction.

[15] I have obviously not treated the matter of *1984*'s sources and analogues in full. There are additional affinities with *Brave New World*, with Cyril Connolly's "Year Nine," and, particularly relevant to Goldstein's book, with Trotsky's *The Revolution Betrayed*. See *Orwell's 1984*, pp. 139–174; John Atkins, *George Orwell* (New York, 1954), pp. 237–241; and George Woodcock, "Utopias in Negative," *Sewanee Review*, LXIV, i (Winter, 1956), 81–97.

[16] In *Collected Essays*, pp. 352–376.

[17] James Burnham, *The Managerial Revolution* (New York, 1941), p. 74.

¹⁸ Burnham, p. 77. In *1984*, the "kind of people" who would "control this world" are "the new aristocracy": ". . . made up for the most part of bureaucrats, scientists, technicians, trade-union organizers, publicity experts, sociologists, teachers, journalists, and professional politicians" (*1984* [New York, 1949], p. 206). Subsequent references are to this edition and are in the text.

¹⁹ "Second Thoughts . . . ," in *Collected Essays*, p. 352. Burnham's divisions in *The Managerial Revolution* are found on pp. 175–176.

²⁰ "Second Thoughts . . . ," p. 353.

²¹ Chronology is something of a problem in any attempt to see Burnham as a source of *Animal Farm*, as it was in assuming that Zamiatin's two-plus-two could be the source of that image in "Looking Back on the Spanish War." The essay on Burnham was published in 1946; *Animal Farm* was written between November, 1943, and February, 1944. But *The Managerial Revolution* was first published in 1940, and the ostensible subject of Orwell's essay, *The Machiavellians*, was published in 1942. Undoubtedly, Orwell had known Burnham's books for some time prior to the writing of his essay: The title, "Second Thoughts . . . ," implies earlier thoughts. (I do not know if any first thoughts are in print.) I think one can reasonably assume Burnham back of the concept of evil and capability in *Animal Farm*.

²² "Second Thoughts . . . ," p. 372. It should be remarked that this is an unfair extension of Burnham's idea, which is only that political behavior is different from other kinds of behavior. However, it is what Orwell believes that is important here.

²³ "Second Thoughts . . . ," p. 368.

²⁴ The question of whether *1984* is in fact prophecy has been much discussed. Generally, the critical consensus has maintained that the world described in the book is exaggerated portrayal rather than futuristic prophecy. "The world of 1984 is the world of 1944, but dirtier and more cruel—and with all the endurance and nobility which distinguished mankind in that upheaval, mysteriously drained away" (Hopkinson, p. 33). Among those critics who share this assessment are Voorhees: "*Nineteen Eighty-Four* is, in countless details, a

realistic picture of the totalitarianism of the present" (p. 87); Richard Rees: "Orwell is merely exaggerating the tendencies he observed in the world of his day" (*George Orwell: Fugitive From the Camp of Victory* [London, 1961], p. 97); Laurence Brander, *George Orwell* (London, 1954), p. 188; Robert Gleckner, "1984 or 1948?" *College English*, XVIII (November, 1956), 95–99; and Atkins, p. 252.

[25] Some descriptions of Flory's existence are strikingly similar to Winston's. E.g., "It is a world in which every thought is censored"; "Free speech is unthinkable"; "So he had learned to live inwardly, secretly, in books and secret thoughts that could not be uttered." (*Burmese Days* [New York, 1950], p. 61.)

[26] E.g., D. J. Dooley, "The Limitations of George Orwell," *University of Toronto Quarterly*, XXVIII (April, 1959), 291–299; Emanuel Edrich, "George Orwell and the Satire in Horror," *Texas Studies in Literature and Language*, IV, i (Spring, 1962), 96–108.

[27] Pp. 98–99. The final casual, diffident "and the like" is a masterful touch: in this world, no alteration of value, no perversion of normality is surprising—because there are no norms by which to measure.

[28] George Knox suggests religious parallels to *The Divine Comedy*: e.g., Winston's "sins" against the state correspond to Carnality (his affair with Julia), Avariciousness (Winston collects artifacts from the past); and Pride (his private life away from the telescreens). "*The Divine Comedy in 1984,*" *Western Humanities Review*, IX, iv (Autumn, 1955), 371–372.

[29] This scene suggests an unremarked source of *1984*. *Under Western Eyes* employs an almost identical technique. The first part of that book ends with Mikulin's unanswered "Where to?" in reply to Razumov's statement that he is leaving and will not be involved in the political intrigues of the Secret Police. The scene is continued and the question answered only at the beginning of the fourth part, with the obvious purpose of dramatic suspense being nicely achieved. And Orwell's intentions reportedly were, just before his death, "to write on Joseph Conrad, whose studies of revolutionaries in such works as *Under Western Eyes* greatly interested him."

(Christopher Hollis, *A Study of George Orwell: The Man and His Works* [London, 1956], p. 207.)

30 Howe, p. 249.

31 E.g., Laurence Brander, *George Orwell* (London, 1954), pp. 191–193. A more interesting case is that of Richard J. Voorhees. In an early article, he sees Winston's faith in the proles as an echo of Orwell's faith in the ordinary Englishman. His concluding remark is that the subtitle of *The Lion and the Unicorn* is "Socialism and the English Genius," as if the subtitle clinches the argument ("*1984*: No Failure of Nerve," *College English*, XVIII, iv [November, 1956]). But by the time of his interesting and insightful book on Orwell (*The Paradox of George Orwell*), Voorhees studiously ignores this point. The proles are not mentioned in the section dealing with *1984*; and in the section "Socialism and Nostalgia," dealing with Orwell's social egalitarianism, he does not mention *1984*.

32 Howe, p. 250.

33 P. 51. It is notable that the last sentence of *1984*, in "The Principles of Newspeak" Appendix, reiterates this date as "the final adoption of Newspeak" (p. 314). The question of whether the novel is portrayal or prophecy seems to me to center here: 1984 is the year of portrayal; Orwell prophecies the specific year of completion in the future.

34 George Steiner, *Language and Silence* (New York, 1967), p. x.

VIII. CONCLUSION

1 Robert B. Heilman, "The State of Letters: Critics, Cliches, Anti-Cliches," *The Sewanee Review*, LXXVI, i (Winter, 1968) 145–158.

Bibliography

This bibliography is selective and makes no pretense to completeness in either Orwell's own works or those concerning him. The first part, dealing with Orwell's own writings, gives a general list of his full-length publications, including collections of essays. But these editions contain only a small part of his journalism, essays, reviews, and the like, much of which remains uncollected. And publications such as the edition called *Collected Essays* are in no way what their title pretends, even regarding major essays. This bibliography, however, does list Orwell's novels, indicates their order of appearance, and cites the editions used.

The bibliography of secondary sources is likewise selective. In this section, I have tried to list only the full-length works concerning Orwell and essays and journal publications which are either relevant to the material within this book or seem to me to be in one way or another interesting.

PART I

Orwell, George. *Animal Farm*. New York, 1954. (First published in 1945.)

————, and Reginald Reynolds, eds. *British Pamphleteers*, vol. I. (London, 1948.)

————. *Burmese Days*. New York, 1950. (First published in 1934.)

————. *A Clergyman's Daughter*. New York, n.d. (First published in 1935.)

————. *Collected Essays*. London, 1961.

————. *Coming Up For Air*. New York, 1950. (First published in 1939.)

————. *Critical Essays*. London, 1960.

————. *Dickens, Dali and Others: Studies in Popular Culture*. New York, 1946.

———. *Down and Out in Paris and London*. New York, 1950. (First published in 1933.)

———. *The English People*. London, 1947.

———. *Homage to Catalonia*. New York, 1952. (First published in 1938.)

———. *Keep the Aspidistra Flying*. New York, 1956. (First published in 1936.)

———. *The Lion and the Unicorn: Socialism and the English Genius*. London, 1941.

———. *Nineteen Eighty-Four*. New York, 1949.

———. *The Road to Wigan Pier*. London, 1937.

———. *Shooting an Elephant and Other Essays*. New York, 1950.

———. *Such, Such Were the Joys*. New York, 1953.

PART II

Atkins, John. *George Orwell*. New York, 1954.

Benson, Frederick R. *Writers in Arms: The Literary Impact of the Spanish Civil War*. New York, 1967.

Brander, Laurence. *George Orwell*. London, 1954.

Cook, Richard. "Rudyard Kipling and George Orwell," *Modern Fiction Studies*, VII, ii (Summer, 1961), 125–135.

Dooley, D. J. "Limitations of George Orwell," *University of Toronto Quarterly*, XXVIII, iii (April, 1959), 291–299.

Dyson, A. E. "Orwell: Irony as Prophecy," in *The Crazy Fabric: Essays in Irony*. London, 1965, pp. 197–219.

Edrich, Emanuel. "George Orwell and the Satire in Horror," *Texas Studies in Literature and Language*, IV, i (Spring, 1962), 96–108.

———. "Naivete and Simplicity in Orwell's Writing: Homage to Catalonia," *University of Kansas City Review*, XXVII, iv (Summer, 1961), 289–297.

Elliott, George P. "George Orwell," in *A Piece of Lettuce*. New York, 1964, pp. 161–170.

Elsbree, Langdon. "The Structured Nightmare of *1984*," *Twentieth Century Literature*, V, iii (October, 1959), 135–141.

Fixler, Michael. "George Orwell and the Instrument of Language," *Iowa English Yearbook*, No. 9 (Fall, 1964), 46–54.

Ford, Hugh D. *A Poet's War: British Poets and the Spanish Civil War.* Philadelphia, 1965.

Fyvel, T. R. "A Case for George Orwell?" *Twentieth Century,* CLX (September, 1956), 254–259.

Gerber, Richard. "Overseas Viewpoint: the English Island Myth," *Critical Quarterly,* I, i (Spring, 1959), 36–43.

Gleckner, Robert F. "1984 or 1948?" *College English,* XVIII, ii (November, 1956), 95–99.

Greenblatt, Stephen Jay. *Three Modern Satirists: Waugh, Orwell, and Huxley.* New Haven and London, 1956.

Harris, Harold J. "Orwell's Essays and *1984,*" *Twentieth Century Literature,* IV, iv (January, 1959), 154–161.

Harrison, John R. *The Reactionaries: A Study of the Anti-Democratic Intelligentsia.* New York, 1967.

Heppenstall, Rayner. *Four Absentees.* London, 1960.

Hoffman, Frederick J. *The Mortal No: Death and the Modern Imagination.* Princeton, New Jersey, 1964.

Hollis, Christopher. *A Study of George Orwell: The Man and His Works.* London, 1956.

Hopkinson, Tom. "Animal Farm," *World Review,* new series 16 (June, 1950), 54–57.

————. *George Orwell,* Writers and Their Work Series No. 39. London, 1962.

Howe, Irving, ed. *Orwell's Nineteen Eighty-Four: Text, Sources, Criticism.* New York, 1963.

————. *Politics and the Novel.* New York, 1957.

Karl, Frederick R. *A Reader's Guide to the Contemporary English Novel.* New York, 1962.

King, Carlyle. "The Politics of George Orwell," *University of Toronto Quarterly,* XXVI, i (October, 1956), 79–91.

Knox, George. "The Divine Comedy in *1984,*" *Western Humanities Review,* IX, iv (Autumn, 1955), 371–372.

Leavis, Q. D. "The Literary Life Respectable. II: George Orwell," *Scrutiny,* IX, ii (September, 1940), 173–176.

Lewis, Wyndham. "Orwell, or Two and Two Make Four," in *The Writer and the Absolute.* London, 1952, pp. 153–198.

Lutman, Stephen. "Orwell's Patriotism," *Journal of Contemporary History,* II, ii (April, 1967), 149–158.

Lyons, John. "George Orwell's Opaque Glass in 1984," Wisconsin Studies in Contemporary Literature, II, iii (Fall, 1961), 39–46.

Macdonald, Dwight. "The British Genius," Partisan Review, IX, ii (March-April, 1942), 166–169.

Mander, John. The Writer and Commitment. London, 1961.

Muste, John M. Say That We Saw Spain Die: Literary Consequences of the Spanish Civil War. Seattle, 1966.

Quintana, Ricardo. "George Orwell: The Satiric Resolution," Wisconsin Studies in Contemporary Literature, II, i (Winter, 1961), 31–38.

Rahv, Phillip. "The Unfuture of Utopia," Partisan Review, XVI, vii (July, 1949), 743–749.

Rees, Richard. George Orwell: Fugitive From the Camp of Victory. London, 1961.

Rieff, Phillip. "George Orwell and the Post-Liberal Imagination," Kenyon Review, XVI, i (Summer, 1954), 49–70.

Rosenfeld, Isaac. "Decency and Death," in An Age of Enormity. Cleveland and New York, 1962, pp. 251–257.

Rovere, Richard, ed. The Orwell Reader. New York, 1959.

Slater, Joseph. "The Fictional Values of 1984," in Rudolf Kirk and C. W. Main, eds., Essays in Literary History: Presented to J. Milton French. New Brunswick, New Jersey, 1961, pp. 249–264.

Thomas, Edward M. Orwell, Writers and Critics Series. London, 1965.

Thomas, Hugh. The Spanish Civil War. New York, 1963.

Voorhees, Richard J. The Paradox of George Orwell. Lafayette, Indiana, 1961.

_____. "Orwell's Secular Crusade," Commonweal, LXI (January 28, 1955), 448–451.

_____. "1984: No Failure of Nerve," College English, XVIII, ii (November, 1956), 101–102.

Wadsworth, Frank W. "Orwell as a Novelist: The Early Work," University of Kansas City Review, XXII, ii (Winter, 1955), 93–99.

_____. "Orwell as a Novelist: The Middle Period," University of Kansas City Review, XXII, iii (Spring, 1956), 189–194.

_____. "Orwell as a Novelist: Orwell's Later Work," Uni-

versity of Kansas City Review, XXII, iv (Summer, 1956), 285–290.

Wain, John. "George Orwell (I)," and "George Orwell (II)," in *Essays on Literature and Ideas*. London, 1963, pp. 180–193, 194–213.

Weintraub, Stanley. *The Last Great Cause: The Intellectuals and The Spanish Civil War*. New York, 1968.

West, Anthony. "George Orwell," in *Principles and Persuasions*. New York, 1951, pp. 164–176.

Williams, Raymond. *Culture and Society 1780–1950*. London, 1958.

Willison, Ian. "Orwell's Bad Good Books," *Twentieth Century*, CLVII, 938 (April, 1955), 354–366.

Wolheim, Richard. "Orwell Reconsidered," *Partisan Review*, XXVII, i (Winter, 1960), 82–97.

Woodcock, George. *The Crystal Spirit: A Study of George Orwell*, Boston, 1966.

––––––. "Utopias in Negative," *Sewanee Review*, LXIV, i (Winter, 1956), 81–97.

World Review, new series 16 (June, 1950). (Orwell memorial issue.)

Zeke, Zoltan G., and William White. "George Orwell: A Selected Bibliography," *Bulletin of Bibliography*, XXIII, v (May-August, 1961), 110–114.

Index